D1527009

EXPLORERS OF ANTIQUITY

FROM ALEXANDER THE GREAT TO MARCO POLO

EXPLORERS OF ANTIQUITY

FROM ALEXANDER THE GREAT TO MARCO POLO

EDITED BY KENNETH PLETCHER, SENIOR EDITOR, GEOGRAPHY

Britannica®
Educational Publishing

IN ASSOCIATION WITH

ROSEN
EDUCATIONAL SERVICES

Published in 2014 by Britannica Educational Publishing
(a trademark of Encyclopædia Britannica, Inc.) in association with Rosen Educational Services, LLC
29 East 21st Street, New York, NY 10010.

First Edition

Britannica Educational Publishing
J.E. Luebering: Director, Core Reference Group
Adam Augustyn: Assistant Manager, Core Reference Group
Marilyn L. Barton: Senior Coordinator, Production Control
Steven Bosco: Director, Editorial Technologies
Lisa S. Braucher: Senior Producer and Data Editor
Yvette Charboneau: Senior Copy Editor
Kathy Nakamura: Manager, Media Acquisition
Kenneth Pletcher, Senior Editor, Geography

Rosen Educational Services
Jeanne Nagle: Senior Editor
Nelson Sá: Art Director
Cindy Reiman: Photography Manager
Marty Levick: Photo Researcher
Brian Garvey: Designer, Cover Design
Introduction by Laura Loria

Library of Congress Cataloging-in-Publication Data

Explorers of antiquity: from Alexander the Great to Marco Polo/edited by Kenneth Pletcher.
    p. cm.—(Britannica guide to explorers and adventurers)
"In association with Britannica Educational Publishing, Rosen Educational Services."
Includes bibliographical references and index.
ISBN 978-1-62275-018-4 (library binding)
1. Explorers—History. 2. Explorers—Biography. I. Pletcher, Kenneth.
G200.B75 2013
910.92'2—dc23

                                                        2012045152

Manufactured in the United States of America

On the cover: Footprints marking the path of travellers across the desert sands of the Sahara. Ancient explorers traveled over harsh terrain such as this, as well as through uncharted waters, in their quest for adventure, knowledge, and glory. *Galyna Andrushko/ Shutterstock.com*

Cover, p. iii (ornamental graphic) © iStockphoto.com/Angelgild; interior pages (scroll) © iStockphoto.com/U.P. Images, (background texture) © iStockphoto.com/Peter Zelei

CONTENTS

16

72

75

94

117

125

INTRODUCTION

A t the earliest time in written history, people's knowledge of the world was limited largely to their own locales. Exploration beyond known frontiers was hampered by natural obstacles, such as rough terrain and weather extremes, as well as the immediate need to provide the basic essentials of food, water, and shelter. As these obstacles were overcome, the known world came to be defined in greater detail, gradually growing outward from centres in the Middle East and South and East Asia to Europe, Africa, and, eventually, the Americas. Over the course of several thousand years, virtually everything that had been known about the world was revised multiple times. This is thanks in large part to the courageous voyagers who ventured into unknown regions, encountering new lands and cultures.

Explorers of Antiquity describes in detail the adventures and discoveries of the first waves of these travelers (from ancient times through the 14th century), whose early probings beyond the known and familiar began the great quest for adventure and discovery that continues to this day. The motivation for some of these daring individuals was conquest,

Bas-relief etching of an ancient sailing vessel, found on a sarcophagus in Lebanon. Leemage/Universal Images Group/ Getty Images

the acquisition of land to enlarge empires and increase their personal power. Others were fueled by a curiosity about the wider world and its people. The desire to practice one's religious beliefs and convert others drove still more to leave home for distant lands. Often these travelers were away for many years; sometimes they never returned. Fortunately for future generations, many of them recorded their exploits, firing the imaginations of those who read them and inspiring countless others to continue pushing back the boundaries of the unknown ever farther.

Wresting control of land, along with the people and resources on it, was a demonstration of power for a nation or tribe. The Cartheginian Hanno explored and colonized the western coast of Africa, founding six cities in or near present-day Morocco during the 5th century BCE. Egyptian rulers Hatsheput (a female king) and Necho II each scored military victories during their respective reigns that broadened their domains. The Celts roamed Europe, from west to east, invading Rome in 390 BCE and parts of Gaul (modern-day France) in the late 2nd century BCE. Forced to migrate farther westward as Germanic tribes invaded their stronghold, the Celts settled in Britain in the 1st century BCE.

Alexander the Great, king of Macedonia from 336 until 323 BCE, was the earliest known large-scale empire builder in the Western world. Ascending his throne after being exiled, he immediately killed his enemies and destroyed rival city-states in a show of force. In 334 BCE he embarked on his great expedition against the Persian Empire with an entourage of 35,000 men that included engineers, architects, scientists, and historians as well as troops. After conquering western Persia and driving King Darius III from his military encampment at Issus (in present-day southern Turkey) in 333 BCE, Alexander continued his conquest southward along the Mediterranean coast and into Egypt. Alexander returned from Egypt to again push eastward into Persian territory, and after Darius's death in 330 BCE, continued on toward India, despite growing acrimony from within his own ranks. After an arduous journey he reached northern India before turning back westward to consolidate his empire. Alexander established dozens of cities in addition to conquering vast territories. In the process of setting up administrations in those areas he was willing to improvise and adapt to local conditions, drawing on a wealth of knowledge of the areas he invaded. In doing so, he set a pattern for future empire builders.

Alexander the Great demonstrated that exploration need not be confined to the discovery—and conquest—of new territory but could also include the consolidation of previously scattered people under a central government and the development of their resources. Best remembered for his oratory and leadership in establishing imperial Rome, Julius Caesar also can be considered an explorer because of his conquest of Gaul. Incorporating those acquired territories into greater Rome gave him the resources needed to continue the expansion and organization of the empire. Caesar's accomplishments and those of his successors contributed significantly to the survival of the Greco-Roman world against invaders for hundreds of years.

In early 13th-century eastern Asia, a dichotomy existed between China, with its centuries-old established culture and succession of centralized dynasties, and Mongolia, an assortment of nomadic and semi-nomadic tribes that formed a shifting, politically loose confederation. The leadership of Genghis

Khan served to unite the Mongolian tribes and drive their expansion beyond the Mongolian steppes. With each victory Genghis drew closer to ever-more sophisticated forms of conquest than simply raiding, destroying, and plundering, wherein he adopted the most useful values and traditions of the peoples and cultures he usurped. One of his Mongol rivals taught him the value of literacy; from others he learned military techniques that he employed to vanquish towns and cities. Indeed, it was during his conquest of the eastern part of Khwārezm in Central Asia that he learned the value of towns, whose inhabitants could then produce goods and taxes to better the economic stability of his empire. By subduing the Jin empire in northern China and then capturing Beijing, Ghengis not only expanded his kingdom but set the stage for his successors to conquer all of China.

Expanding human knowledge of the physical world was a goal of some explorers. Around 300 BCE, Pytheas became the first Greek to travel to Britain via the Mediterranean Sea. In the process, he recorded reasonably accurate measurements of Britain's circumference and its distance from Massalia (now Marseille, France) and included notes about local practices along with his scientific observations. The 12th-century geographer al Sharīf al–Idrīsī created a map of the world and a geographic text intended as a key to the map for his patron, King Roger II of Sicily. As part of this project, he personally traveled to western Europe and Asia Minor (modern Turkey), while sending others, including artists, to other parts of the world to record and draw what they observed there. His completed works, though flawed, are considered one of the greatest works of medieval geography.

The desire to become more educated about other cultures was a natural consequence of humanity's expanding interest in the world. In 402 CE, Faxian, a Chinese Buddhist monk, undertook a pilgrimage to India in order to visit the sites most associated with the Buddha's life and teaching, as well as what were then the seats of Buddhist knowledge. He journeyed forth by land and returned by sea, encountering severe weather that delayed his return. He brought back with him Buddhist texts that he translated from Sanskrit to Chinese. More than two hundred years later, another Buddhist monk from China, Xuanzang, made a similar trip, also returning with Buddhist texts that he translated into Chinese. Beyond transcription of sacred texts, Xuanzang also wrote an extensive and detailed account of his journey. His *Datang-Xiyu-Ji* ("Records of the Western Regions of the Great Tang Dynasty") held audiences throughout China in its thrall—including the Tang emperor—and has been a great boon to historians for centuries. Among other early explorers traveling in search of religious enlightenment was Rabbi Benjamin of Tudela, whose pioneering travels to China in the 12th century were motivated in part by a desire to seek out Jews in other parts of the world.

Rather than being driven by a desire to learn about other cultures, some early explorers sought to spread their own beliefs and traditions to others. For instance, Leif Eriksson didn't originally set out to discover new worlds. His father, Erik the Red, founded the Norse settlement in Greenland, where the young Leif lived before sailing to Norway in about 1000. Leif was sent back to Greenland by King Olaf I Tryggvason to convert the settlers there to Christianity. He sailed off course, however, and landed somewhere in northeastern North America, possibly northern Newfoundland. Leif was successful in his orginal mission, though, for after returning to Greenland, he converted his mother, who had built the first Christian church on the island—hence, in North America.

In 1245, the Franciscan friar Giovanni da Pian del Carpini was sent by Pope Innocent IV as an emissary of the papacy to the Mongol leadership. Several months after his arrival, political instability forced him to return westward, bringing with him a wealth of knowledge about the Mongols, recorded in his treatise *Liber Tatarorum* ("Book of the Tatars"). Another Franciscan, Giovanni da Montecorvino, was sent to India and China as a missionary, where he met with considerable success. He became the first archbishop of Dadu (now Beijing) and may have converted the Yuan (Mongol) emperor Khaishan. In the next century, Odoric of Pordenone was said to have baptized more than 20,000 people during travels to Persia, Mesopotamia, India, and China that lasted more than a decade.

Most of the explorers and adventurers included in this book wrote journals, accounts, and other documents about their travels and experiences. These historical records have enabled later generations to study the thinking of the times and understand how exploration expanded awareness of the world. Knowledge of some of the earliest explorations, however, exists only in other written records, as happened with Hanno (in a 10th-century Greek manuscript) and Leif Eriksson (in the Icelandic sagas). In other instances, the original writings of some explorers have been lost, yet their stories have been preserved in the accounts of those familiar with their work. Such was the case with Scylax of Caryanda, who was the first Western explorer to write about the geography of the Indian subcontinent. His descriptions are cited by Herodotus, the 5th-century BCE Greek explorer of the Persian Empire. Herodotus himself chronicled the Greek-Persian wars, inserting anecdotes and speeches in his accounts to create a lively narrative that is also an examination of Persian culture and history. Herodotus' writings are noted for their impartiality, detail, and humanistic slant.

In the 9th and 10th centuries, a number of explorers from the Middle East produced written works about their expeditions. A noted philologist—someone who studies written texts—as well as an explorer, Eldad the Danite was inspired by his travels to North Africa and Spain to write his own work, the Hebrew narrative *Sefer Eldad*. The writings of al-Mas'ūdī, detailing his trips from Iraq to Syria, Iran, Armenia, Sri Lanka, and East Africa, were vast tomes combining world history, geography, and political and sociological observation. His sources were often ordinary people, such as merchants, whose information he transcribed without comment. Al-Mas'ūdī later condensed his works, making them more accessible and thereby expanding their influence. Yemeni-born author al-Hamdānī produced *Al-lkl īl*, an examination of Saudi Arabian genealogy, topography, and history, after spending most of his life traveling the region. He included a collection of poetry as well.

The son of wealthy Venetian traders, Marco Polo spent much of his life traveling throughout Asia. After trading with and living among the Mongols for years, Marco's father and uncle gained the confidence of the great khan Kublai (who by then was the emperor of Yuan-dynasty China) and returned to the Venetian court as Kublai's ambassadors. Along with his uncle and father, Polo spent some 17 years in the Yuan empire, where he was sent on fact-finding missions to locales such as Hangzhou and possibly as far as north-central Myanmar (Burma). The Polos' return to Europe was prompted by the imminent death of the aging Khan and the possibility that they would not enjoy the same level of favour under his successor. The roundabout route home led him through Southeast Asia, Ceylon (Sri Lanka), and Persia. Shortly after his return, Polo was imprisoned by the Genoese, due to his involvement in a sea battle in the Mediterranean. His incarceration turned out to be a fortunate circumstance for historians and future generations of explorers; while in prison he met a writer to whom Polo dictated the tales of his travels. Now known as *Il Milione*, the book was hugely successful at that time and became a valuable resource for historians and later explorers—even though it was marred with inaccuracies and reworkings of the text.

The similarly well-traveled 14th-century Morrocan explorer Ibn Baṭṭūṭah spent much of his life traveling an estimated 75,000 miles (120,000 km) around the Muslim world. After a pilgrimage to Mecca, he was consumed with the idea of seeing every place where Muslims lived. The territory he covered included the Middle East, Central Asia, India (where he was appointed grand qadi of Delhi), and China. His memoirs proved to be highly valuable historical and geographical documents for their scope and details. Ibn Baṭṭūṭah appears to have met more than 60 rulers of various nations, as well as countless other officials and dignitaries.

Today, humans have reached nearly every spot on the globe. In an age when satellite photography and GPS technology makes it possible to create highly detailed and accurate maps, it is difficult to imagine that people once ventured far from home with little or no idea of what they might encounter during their travels. Further, it is amazing that explorers of old spent years away from their homes—often among people who may not have welcomed their presence—pursuing knowledge about new lands and cultures. Their willingness to face hardships and uncertainty in order to obtain the wealth of information they compiled and shared has lain the groundwork for countless future generations of explorers and adventurers.

PHOENICIANS

PHOENICIANS

Phoenicia was an ancient region along the eastern Mediterranean Sea corresponding to modern Lebanon, with adjoining parts of modern Syria and Israel. Its inhabitants, the Phoenicians, were notable merchants, traders, and colonizers of the Mediterranean region in the 1st millennium BCE. The chief cities of Phoenicia (excluding colonies) were Sidon, Tyre, and Berot (modern Beirut).

It is not certain what the Phoenicians called themselves in their own language; it appears to have been Kena'ani (Akkadian: Kinahna), "Canaanites." In Hebrew the word *kena'ani* has the secondary meaning of "merchant," a term that well characterizes the Phoenicians. The Phoenicians probably arrived in the area about 3000 BCE. Nothing is known of their original homeland, though some traditions place it in the region of the Persian Gulf.

At the ancient Phoenician city of Byblos, commercial and religious connections with Egypt are attested from the Egyptian 4th dynasty (*c.* 2613–*c.* 2494 BCE). Extensive trade was certainly carried on by the 16th century, and the Egyptians soon established suzerainty (overlordship) over much of Phoenicia. The 14th century, however, was one of much political unrest, and Egypt eventually lost its hold over the area. Beginning in the 9th century, the independence of Phoenicia was increasingly threatened by the advance of Assyria, the kings of which several times exacted tribute and took control of parts or all

Model of a Phoenician ship, 13th century BCE. Courtesy of the
Museum of the Philadelphia Civic Center

of Phoenicia. In 538 Phoenicia passed under the rule of the Persians. The country was later taken by Alexander the Great and in 64 BCE was incorporated into the Roman province of Syria; Aradus, Sidon, and Tyre, however, retained self-government. The oldest form of government in the Phoenician cities seems to have been kingship, which was limited by the power of the wealthy merchant families. Federation of the cities on a large scale never seems to have occurred.

The Phoenicians were well known to their contemporaries as sea traders and colonizers, and by the 2nd millennium they had already extended their influence along the coast of the Levant by a series of settlements, including Joppa (Jaffa, modern Tel Aviv–Yafo, Israel), Dor, Acre, and Ugarit. Colonization of areas in North Africa (e.g., Carthage), Anatolia (Asia Minor), and Cyprus also occurred at an early date. Carthage, in what is now Tunisia, became the chief maritime and commercial power in the western Mediterranean. Several smaller Phoenician settlements were planted as stepping stones along the route to Spain and its mineral wealth. Phoenician exports included cedar and pine wood, fine linen from Tyre, Byblos, and Berytos, cloths dyed with the famous Tyrian purple (made from a snail of the genus *Murex*), embroideries from Sidon, wine, metalwork and glass, glazed faience (glazed earthenware), salt, and dried fish. In addition, the Phoenicians conducted an important transit trade.

LAPITA PEOPLE

The Lapita people were members of a cultural complex of the Pacific Ocean islands and were presumably the original human settlers of Melanesia, much of Polynesia, and parts of Micronesia. The complex is dated to between 1600 and 500 BCE. The Lapita culture is named for a type of fired pottery that was first extensively investigated at the site of Lapita in New Caledonia.

The Lapita people were originally from Taiwan and other regions of East Asia. They were highly mobile seaborne explorers and colonists who had established themselves on the Bismarck Archipelago (northeast of New Guinea) by 2000 BCE. Beginning about 1600 BCE they spread to the Solomon Islands and had reached Fiji, Tonga, and the rest of western Polynesia by 1000 BCE, further dispersing to Micronesia by 500 BCE.

The Lapita people are known principally on the basis of the remains of their fired pottery, which consists of beakers, cooking pots, and bowls. Many of the pottery shards that have been found are decorated with geometric designs made by stamping the unfired clay with a tooth-like implement. A few shards with figurative designs have also been found. Lapita pottery has been found from New Guinea eastward to Samoa. Fishhooks, pieces of obsidian and chert flakes, and beads and rings made of shells are the other principal artifacts of the Lapita culture.

The Lapita appear to have been skilled sailors and navigators who subsisted largely, but not entirely, by fishing along the coasts of the islands on which they lived. They

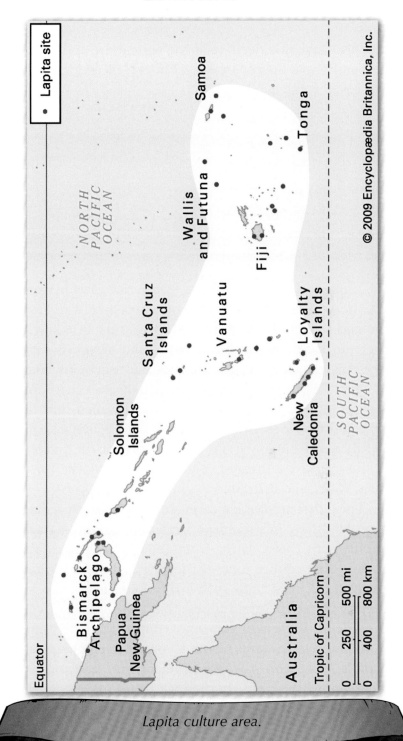

Lapita culture area.

may also have practiced domestic agriculture and animal husbandry to a limited extent, although the evidence for this remains fragmentary.

THE CELTS

The Celts (also spelled Kelts, Latin: *Celtae*) were members of an early Indo-European people who from the 2nd millennium BCE to the 1st century BCE spread over much of Europe. Their tribes and groups eventually ranged from the British Isles and northern Spain to as far east as Transylvania, the Black Sea coasts, and Galatia in Anatolia and were in part absorbed into the Roman Empire as Britons, Gauls, Boii, Galatians, and Celtiberians. Linguistically they survive in the modern Celtic speakers of Ireland, Highland Scotland, the Isle of Man, Wales, and Brittany.

The oldest archaeological evidence of the Celts comes from Hallstatt, Austria, near Salzburg. Excavated graves of chieftains there, dating from about 700 BCE, exhibit an Iron Age culture (one of the first in Europe), which received in Greek trade such luxury items as bronze and pottery vessels. It would appear that these wealthy Celts, based from Bavaria to Bohemia, controlled trade routes along the river systems of the Rhône, Seine, Rhine, and Danube, and were the predominant and unifying element among the Celts. In their westward movement the Hallstatt warriors overran Celtic peoples of their own kind, incidentally introducing the use of iron, one of the reasons for their own overlordship.

For the centuries after the establishment of trade with the Greeks, the archaeology of the Celts can be followed with greater precision. By the mid-5th century BCE the La Tène culture, with its distinctive art style of abstract geometric designs and stylized bird and animal forms, had begun to emerge among the Celts centred on the middle Rhine, where trade with the Etruscans of central Italy, rather than with the Greeks, was

Bronze bucket found at early Iron Age cemetery at Hallstatt, Austria, about 6th century BCE. Courtesy of the trustees of the British Museum

becoming predominant. Between the 5th and 1st centuries BCE the La Tène culture accompanied the migrations of Celtic tribes into eastern Europe and westward into the British Isles.

Although Celtic bands probably had penetrated into northern Italy from earlier times, the year 400 BCE is generally accepted as the approximate date for the beginning of the great invasion of migrating Celtic tribes whose names Insubres, Boii, Senones, and Lingones were recorded by later Latin historians. Rome was sacked by Celts about 390; raiding bands wandered throughout the whole peninsula and reached Sicily. The Celtic territory south of the Alps where they settled came to be known as Cisalpine Gaul (Gallia Cisalpina). The area's warlike inhabitants remained an ever-constant menace to Rome until their defeat at Telamon in 225.

Dates associated with the Celts in their movement into the Balkans are 335 BCE, when Alexander the Great received delegations of Celts living near the Adriatic, and 279 BCE, when Celts sacked Delphi in Greece but suffered defeat at the hands of the Aetolians. In the following year, three Celtic tribes crossed the Bosporus into Anatolia and created widespread havoc. By 276 BCE they had settled in parts of Phrygia but continued raiding and pillaging until finally quelled by Attalus I of Pergamum about 230 BCE. In Italy, meanwhile, Rome had established supremacy over the whole of Cisalpine Gaul by 192 and, in 124 BCE, had conquered territory beyond the western Alps—in what became part of the *provincia* of Transalpine Gaul (Gallia Transalpina; modern-day Provence).

The final episodes of Celtic independence were enacted in Transalpine Gaul, the *provincia* having expanded to encompass the whole territory from the Rhine River and the Alps westward to the Atlantic Ocean. The threat was twofold: Germanic tribes pressing westward toward and across the Rhine, and the Roman arms in the south poised for further annexations. The Germanic onslaught was first felt in Bohemia, the land of the Boii, and in Noricum, a Celtic kingdom in the eastern Alps. The German assailants were known as the Cimbri, a people generally thought to have originated in Jutland (Denmark). A Roman army sent to the relief of Noricum in 113 BCE was defeated, and thereafter the Cimbri, now joined by the Teutoni, ravaged widely in Transalpine Gaul, overcoming all Gaulish and Roman resistance. On attempting to enter Italy, these German marauders were finally routed by Roman armies in 102 and 101 BCE. There is no doubt that, during this period, many Celtic tribes formerly living east of the Rhine were forced to seek refuge west of the river, and these migrations, as well as further German threats, gave Julius Caesar the opportunity (58 BCE) to begin the campaigns that led to the Roman annexation of the whole of Gaul.

The Celtic settlement of Britain and Ireland is deduced mainly from archaeological and linguistic considerations. The only direct historical source for the identification of an insular people with the Celts is Caesar's report of the migration of Belgic tribes to Britain, but the inhabitants of both islands were regarded by the Romans as closely related to the Gauls.

Information on Celtic institutions is available from various classical authors and from the body of ancient Irish literature. The social system of the tribe, or "people," was threefold: king, warrior aristocracy, and freemen farmers. The druids, who were occupied with magico-religious duties, were recruited from families of the warrior class but ranked higher. Thus Caesar's distinction between *druides* (man of religion and learning), *eques* (warrior), and *plebs* (commoner) is fairly apt. As in other Indo-European systems, the family was patriarchal. The basic economy of the Celts was mixed farming, and, except in times of unrest, single farmsteads were usual. Owing to the wide variations in terrain and climate, cattle raising was more important than cereal cultivation in some regions. Hill forts provided places of refuge, but warfare was generally open and consisted of single challenges and combat as much as of general fighting. Artifacts of the La Tène culture (named for the La Tène archaeological site in western Switzerland) give witness to the aesthetic qualities of the Celts, and they greatly prized music and many forms of oral literary composition.

HATSHEPSUT

(fl. 15th century BCE)

H atshepsut (or Hatchepsut) was a female king of Egypt (reigned in her own right c. 1473–58 BCE) who attained unprecedented power for a woman, adopting the full titles and regalia of a pharaoh.

Hatshepsut, the elder daughter of the 18th-dynasty king Thutmose I and his consort Ahmose, was married to her half brother Thutmose II, son of the lady Mutnofret. Since three of Mutnofret's older sons had died prematurely, Thutmose II inherited his father's throne about 1492 BCE, with Hatshepsut as his consort. Hatshepsut bore one daughter, Neferure, but no son. When her husband died about 1479 BCE, the throne passed to his son Thutmose III, born to Isis, a lesser harem queen. As Thutmose III was an infant, Hatshepsut acted as regent for the young king.

For the first few years of her stepson's reign, Hatshepsut was an entirely conventional regent. But by the end of his seventh regnal year, she had been crowned king and adopted a full royal titulary (the royal protocol adopted by Egyptian sovereigns). Hatshepsut and Thutmose III were now corulers of Egypt, with Hatshepsut very much the dominant king. Hitherto Hatshepsut had been depicted as a typical queen, with a female body and appropriately feminine garments. But now, after a brief period of experimentation that involved combining a female body with

Drawing showing an Egyptian ship being loaded in advance of an expedition to the Land of Punt during Hatshepsut's reign. Mansell/Time & Life Pictures/Getty Images

kingly (male) regalia, her formal portraits began to show Hatshepsut with a male body, wearing the traditional regalia of kilt, crown or head-cloth, and false beard. To dismiss this as a serious attempt to pass herself off as a man is to misunderstand Egyptian artistic convention, which showed things not as they were but as they should be. In causing herself to be depicted as a traditional king, Hatshepsut ensured that this is what she would become.

Hatshepsut never explained why she took the throne or how she persuaded Egypt's elite to accept her new position. However, an essential element of her success was a group of loyal officials, many handpicked, who controlled all the key positions in her government. Most prominent among these was Senenmut, overseer of all royal works and tutor to Neferure. Some observers have suggested that Hatshepsut and Senenmut may have been lovers, but there is no evidence to support this claim.

Traditionally, Egyptian kings defended their land against the enemies who lurked at Egypt's borders. Hatshepsut's reign was essentially a peaceful one, and her foreign policy was based on trade rather than war. But scenes on the walls of her Dayr al-Baḥrī temple, in western Thebes, suggest that she began with a short, successful military campaign in Nubia. More-complete scenes show Hatshepsut's seaborne trading expedition on the Red Sea to Punt, a trading centre (since vanished) on the East African coast beyond the southernmost end of the sea. Gold, ebony, animal skins, baboons, processed myrrh, and living myrrh trees were brought back to Egypt, and the trees were planted in the gardens of Dayr al-Baḥrī.

NECHO II

(fl. 7th century BCE)

Necho II was a king of Egypt (reigned 610–595 BCE), a member of the 26th dynasty. He unsuccessfully attempted to aid Assyria against the Neo-Babylonians and later sponsored an expedition that circumnavigated Africa.

According to the Greek historian Herodotus, Necho began the construction of a canal from the Nile River to the Red Sea, probably in response to the growth of trade in the Egyptian Delta, but an oracle persuaded him to discontinue the project. A threat developed in Mesopotamia, where the Assyrian Empire was falling to the Babylonians. Necho ordered fleets to be built on the Mediterranean and Red seas, and with them he undertook a Syrian campaign in 608 BCE to assist the battered Assyrian armies. When Josiah, king of Judah and an ally of the Neo-Babylonians, was slain in battle at Megiddo, Necho replaced Josiah's chosen successor with his own nominee and imposed tribute on Judah. In 606 the Egyptians routed the Neo-Babylonians, but at the great Battle of Carchemish (a Syrian city on the middle Euphrates River) in 605 the Neo-Babylonian crown prince, Nebuchadrezzar, soundly defeated Necho's troops and forced their withdrawal from Syria and Palestine. Egypt itself was threatened in 601, but Necho repelled the enemy and continued to promote anti-Babylonian coalitions in Syria and Palestine.

Herodotus also reports that Necho sent an expedition to circumnavigate Africa. His navigators apparently accomplished the feat, for they reported that, after a certain point in their voyage, the sun lay to their right (i.e., northward) as they sailed around southern Africa.

SCYLAX OF CARYANDA

(fl. 6th century BCE)

S cylax of Caryanda was an ancient Greek explorer who was a pioneer in geography and the first Western observer to give an account of India.

It is known from Herodotus that Scylax was sent by the Persian king Darius I (in about 515 BCE) to explore the course of the Indus River and that he returned by sea after two and a half years to the Isthmus of Heroonpolis (Suez). References in ancient authorities seem to show that he left a record of his voyages, but none of the references is even nearly contemporary; and it is difficult to say in what manner knowledge of Scylax was transmitted. The few fragments suggest a work in the form of a *Periplus* (mariner's coastal guide), with some geographic and ethnographic description and, in the account of India, some element of the fabulous. The extant *Periplus* that has come down under his name cannot, however, be the work of Scylax of Caryanda. Another work doubtfully attributed to Scylax is a work on the Carian Heraclides of Mylasa, who distinguished himself in the Greek revolt against the Persians (498 BCE) and possibly in the second Greco-Persian War (480 BCE). That the explorer and geographer was a pioneer also in historical-biographical literature is improbable.

HERODOTUS

(b. 484 BCE?, Halicarnassus, Asia Minor [now Bodrum, Turkey]?—d. 430–420)

Herodotus was an intrepid Greek traveler and the author of the first great narrative history produced in the ancient world, the *History*, which was a chronicle of the Greco-Persian Wars.

It is believed that Herodotus was born at Halicarnassus, a Greek city in southwest Asia Minor (Anatolia) that was then under Persian rule. The precise dates of his birth and death are alike uncertain. He is thought to have resided in Athens and to have met Sophocles and then to have left for Thurii, a new colony in southern Italy sponsored by Athens. The latest event alluded to in his *History* belongs to 430 BCE, but how soon after or where he died is not known. There is good reason to believe that he was in Athens, or at least in central Greece, during the early years of the Peloponnesian War, from 431, and that his work was published and known there before 425.

Herodotus was a wide traveler. His longer wandering covered a large part of the Persian Empire: he went to Egypt, at least as far south as the island of Elephantine (Aswān), and he also visited Libya, Syria, Babylonia, Susa in Elam, Lydia, and Phrygia. He journeyed up the Hellespont to Byzantium, went to Thrace and Macedonia, and traveled northward to beyond the Danube River and to Scythia eastward along the northern shores of the Black Sea as far as the Don River and some way inland. These travels would have taken many years.

STRUCTURE AND SCOPE OF THE *HISTORY*

Herodotus' subject in his *History* is the wars between Greece and Persia (499–479 BCE) and their preliminaries. As it has survived, the *History* is divided into nine books (the division is not Herodotus' own): Books I–V describe the background to the Greco-Persian Wars; Books VI–IX contain the history of the wars, culminating in an account of the Persian king Xerxes' invasion of Greece (Book VII) and the great Greek victories at Salamis, Plataea, and

HERODOTVS

Statue of the ancient Greek traveler Herodotus, situated along the balustrade of the Library of Congress Thomas Jefferson Building, Washington, D.C. Library of Congress Prints and Photographs Division

Mycale in 480–479 BCE. There are two parts in the *History*, one being the systematic narrative of the war of 480–479 with its preliminaries from 499 onward (including the Ionic revolt and the Battle of Marathon in Book VI), the other being the story of the growth and organization of the Persian Empire and a description of its geography, social structure, and history.

There has been much debate among modern scholars whether Herodotus from the first had this arrangement in mind or had begun with a scheme for only one part, either a description of Persia or a history of the war, and if so, with which. One likely opinion is that Herodotus began with a plan for the history of the war and that later he decided on a description of the Persian Empire itself. For a man like Herodotus was bound to ask himself what the Persian-led invasion force meant. Herodotus was deeply impressed not only by the great size of the Persian Empire but also by the varied and polyglot nature of its army, which was yet united in a single command, in complete contrast to the Greek forces with their political divisions and disputatious commanders, although the Greeks shared a common language, religion, and way of thought and the same feeling about what they were fighting for. This difference had to be explained to his readers, and to this end he describes the empire.

A logical link between the two main sections is to be found in the account in Book VII of the westward march of Xerxes' immense army from Sardis to the Hellespont on the way to the crossing by the bridge of boats into Greece proper. First comes a story of Xerxes' arrogance and petulance, followed by another of his savage and autocratic cruelty, and then comes a long, detailed description of the separate military contingents of the army marching as if on parade, followed by a detailed enumeration of all the national and racial elements in the huge invasion force.

Herodotus describes the history and constituent parts of the Persian Empire in Books I–IV. His method in the account of the empire is to describe each division of it not in a geographical order but as each was conquered by Persia—by the successive Persian kings Cyrus, Cambyses, and Darius. (The one exception to this arrangement is Lydia, which is treated at the very beginning of the history not because it was first conquered but because it was the first foreign country to attack and overcome the Greek cities of Asia Minor.)

The first section of Book I, the history and description of Lydia and its conquest by the Persians, is followed by the story of Cyrus himself, his defeat of the Medes and a description of Persia proper, his attack on the Massagetae (in the northeast, toward the Caspian), and his death. Book II contains the succession of Cambyses, Cyrus' son, his plan to attack Egypt, and an immensely long account of that unique land and its history. Book III describes the Persians' conquest of Egypt, the failure of their invasions to the south (Ethiopia) and west; the madness and death of Cambyses; the struggles over the succession in Persia, ending with the choice of Darius as the new king; the organization of the vast new empire by him, with some account of the most distant provinces as far east as Bactria and northwest India; and the internal revolts suppressed by Darius. Book IV begins with the description and history of the Scythian peoples, from the Danube to the Don, whom Darius proposed to attack by crossing the Bosporus, and of their land and of the Black Sea.

Then follows the story of the Persian invasion of Scythia, which carried with it the submission of more Greek cities, such as Byzantium; of the Persians' simultaneous attack from Egypt on Libya, which had been colonized by Greeks; and the description of that country and its colonization. Book V describes further Persian advances into Greece proper from the Hellespont and the submission of Thrace and Macedonia and many more Greek cities to Persian might, then the beginning of the revolt of the Greek cities of Ionia against Persia in 499, and so to the main subject of the whole work.

METHOD OF NARRATION

This brief account of the first half of Herodotus' *History* not only conceals its infinite variety but is positively misleading insofar as it suggests a straightforward geographical, sociological, and historical description of a varied empire. The *History*'s structure is more complex than that, and so is Herodotus' method of narration. For example, Herodotus had no need to explain Greek geography, customs, or political systems to his Greek readers, but he did wish to describe the political situation at the relevant times of the many Greek cities later involved in the war. This he achieved by means of digressions skillfully worked into his main narrative. He thus describes the actions of Croesus, the king of Lydia, who conquered the Greeks of mainland Ionia but who was in turn subjugated by the Persians, and this account leads Herodotus into a digression on the past history of the Ionians and Dorians and the division between the two most powerful Greek cities, the Ionian Athens and the Doric Sparta. Athens' complex political development in the 6th century BCE is touched upon, as is the conservative character of the Spartans. All of this, and much besides, some of it only included because of Herodotus' personal interest, helps to explain the positions of these Greek states in 490, the year of the Battle of Marathon, and in 480, the year in which Xerxes invaded Greece.

One important and, indeed, remarkable feature of Herodotus' *History* is his love of and gift for narrating history in the storyteller's manner (which is not unlike Homer's). In this regard he inserts not only amusing short stories but also dialogue and even speeches by the leading historical figures into his narrative, thus beginning a practice that would persist throughout the course of historiography in the classical world.

OUTLOOK ON LIFE

The story of Croesus in Book I gives Herodotus the occasion to foreshadow, as it were, in Croesus' talk with Solon the general meaning of the story of the Greco-Persian Wars, and so of his whole *History*—that great prosperity is "a slippery thing" and may lead to a fall, more particularly if it is accompanied by arrogance and folly as it was in Xerxes. The story of Xerxes' invasion of Greece is a clear illustration of the moral viewpoint here; a war that by all human reasoning should have been won was irretrievably lost. To Herodotus, the old moral "pride comes before a fall" was a matter of common observation and had been proved true by the greatest historical event of his time. Herodotus believes in divine retribution as a punishment of human impiety, arrogance, and cruelty, but his emphasis is always on the actions and character of men, rather than on the interventions of the gods, in his descriptions of historical events. This fundamentally rationalistic approach was an epochal innovation in Western historiography.

QUALITIES AS A HISTORIAN

Herodotus was a great traveler with an eye for detail, a good geographer, a man with an indefatigable interest in the customs and past history of his fellow men, and a man of the widest tolerance, with no bias for the Greeks and against the barbarians. He was neither naive nor easily credulous. It is this which makes the first half of his work not only so readable but of such historical importance. In the second half he is largely, but by no means only, writing military history, and it is evident that he knew little of military matters. Yet he understood at least one essential of the strategy of Xerxes' invasion, the Persians' dependence on their fleet though they came by land, and therefore Herodotus understood the decisive importance of the naval battle at Salamis.

Similarly, in his political summaries he is commonly content with explaining events on the basis of trivial personal motives. Yet here again he understood that the political meaning of the struggle between the great territorial empire of Persia and the small Greek states was not one of Greek independence only but the rule of law as the Greeks understood it. Herodotus also showed a keen understanding that the political importance of the Battle of Marathon for the Greek world was that it foreshadowed the rise of Athens (confirmed by Salamis) to a position of equality and rivalry with Sparta, as well as the end of the long-accepted primacy of the latter. He knew that war was not only a question of victory or defeat, glorious as the Greek victory was, but brought its own consequences in its train, including the internal quarrels and rivalry between the leading Greek city-states, quarreling that was to later culminate in the devastating internecine strife of the Peloponnesian War (431–404 BCE).

HANNO

(fl. 5th century BCE)

The Carthaginian Hanno conducted a voyage of exploration and colonization to the west coast of Africa sometime during the 5th century BCE.

Setting sail with 60 vessels holding 30,000 men and women, Hanno founded Thymiaterion (now Kenitra, Morocco) and built a temple at Soloeis (Cape Cantin, now Cape Meddouza). He then founded five additional cities in and around present Morocco, including Carian Fortress (Greek: Karikon Teichos) and Acra (Agadir). The Carian Fortress is perhaps to be identified with Essaouira on the Moroccan coast, where archaeological remains of Punic settlers have been found.

Farther south Hanno founded Cerne, possibly on the Río de Oro, as a trading post. He evidently reached the coast of present Gambia or Sierra Leone, and may have ventured as far as Cameroon. Modern scholars doubt whether Hanno actually continued beyond Morocco.

An account of Hanno's voyage was written in the temple of Baal at Carthage. The story survives in a 10th-century-CE Greek manuscript known as *Periplus of Hannon*, which claims to be an ancient Greek translation from the Punic inscription.

ALEXANDER THE GREAT

(b. 356 BCE, Pella, Macedonia—d. June 13, 323 BCE, Babylon)

Alexander was the celebrated king of Macedonia (reigned 336–323 BCE) who overthrew the Persian Empire, carried Macedonian arms to India, and laid the foundations for the Hellenistic world of territorial kingdoms. Also known as Alexander III or Alexander of Macedonia, he was the first to combine great charisma and organizational and leadership skills with the desire to seek his fortune in far-off exotic places. Already the subject of fabulous stories in his lifetime, he later became the hero of a full-scale legend bearing only the sketchiest resemblance to his historical career.

EARLY YEARS

Alexander was born in 356 BCE at Pella in Macedonia, the son of King Philip II and Olympias (daughter of King Neoptolemus of Epirus). From age 13 to 16 Alexander was taught by Aristotle, who inspired him with an interest in philosophy, medicine, and scientific investigation. However, the student later advanced beyond his teacher's narrow precept that non-Greeks should be treated as slaves.

Left in charge of Macedonia in 340 during Philip's attack on Byzantium, Alexander defeated the Maedi, a

Thracian people. Two years later he commanded the left wing at the Battle of Chaeronea, in which Philip defeated the allied Greek states, and displayed personal courage in breaking the Sacred Band of Thebes, an elite group of soldiers in the Theban army. A year later Philip divorced Olympias. After a quarrel at a feast held to celebrate his father's new marriage, Alexander and his mother fled to Epirus; Alexander later went to Illyria. Shortly afterward, father and son were reconciled and Alexander returned, but his position as heir was jeopardized.

In 336, however, on Philip's assassination, Alexander, acclaimed by the army, succeeded without opposition. He at once executed the princes of Lyncestis, alleged to be behind Philip's murder, along with all possible rivals and the whole of the faction opposed to him. He then marched south, recovered a wavering Thessaly, and at an assembly of the Greek League at Corinth was appointed generalissimo for the forthcoming invasion of Asia, already planned and initiated by Philip. Returning to Macedonia by way of Delphi (where the Pythian priestess acclaimed him "invincible"), he advanced into Thrace in the spring of 335 BCE and, after forcing the Shipka Pass and crushing the Triballi, crossed the Danube River to disperse the Getae. Turning west, he then defeated and shattered a coalition of Illyrians who had invaded Macedonia.

Meanwhile, a rumour of his death had precipitated a revolt of Theban democrats; other Greek states favoured Thebes, and the Athenians, urged on by Demosthenes, voted help. In 14 days Alexander marched his army some 240 miles (385 km) from Pelion (near modern Korçë, Albania) in Illyria to Thebes. When the Thebans refused to surrender, he made an entry and razed their city to the ground, sparing only temples and the house of lyric poet Pindar. Six thousand were killed, and all survivors were sold into slavery. The other Greek states were cowed by this severity, and therefore Alexander could afford to treat Athens leniently. Macedonian garrisons were left in Corinth, Chalcis, and the Cadmea (the citadel of Thebes).

BEGINNINGS OF THE PERSIAN EXPEDITION

From his accession Alexander had set his mind on the Persian expedition. He had grown up to the idea. Moreover, he needed the wealth of Persia if he was to maintain the army built by Philip and pay off the 500 talents (a form of currency) he owed. The exploits of the Ten Thousand (Greek soldiers of fortune) and Agesilaus of Sparta in successfully campaigning in Persian territory had revealed the vulnerability of the Persian Empire. With a good cavalry force Alexander could expect to defeat any Persian army.

In spring 334 BCE he crossed the Dardanelles, leaving Antipater, who had already faithfully served Alexander's father, as his deputy in Europe with over 13,000 men; he himself commanded about 30,000 foot and over 5,000 cavalry, of whom nearly 14,000 were Macedonians and about 7,000 allies sent by the Greek League. This army was to prove remarkable for its balanced combination of arms. Much work fell on the lightly armed Cretan and Macedonian archers, the Thracians, and the Agrianian javelin men. But in pitched battle the striking force was the cavalry, and the core of the army—should the issue still remain undecided after the cavalry charge—was the 9,000-strong infantry phalanx, armed with 13-foot spears and shields, and the 3,000 men of the royal battalions, the hypaspists.

Alexander's second in command was Parmenio, who had secured a foothold in Asia Minor (Anatolia) during Philip's lifetime; many of his family and supporters were

Mosaic of Alexander the Great discovered in the House of the Faun, Pompeii, Italy. © Alfio Ferlito/Shutterstock.com

entrenched in positions of responsibility. From the outset Alexander seems to have envisaged an unlimited operation. The army was accompanied by surveyors, engineers, architects, scientists, court officials, and historians.

After visiting Ilium (Troy), a romantic gesture inspired by Homer, Alexander confronted his first Persian army, led by three satraps (provincial governors), at the Granicus (modern Kocabaş) River, near the Sea of Marmara in May/June 334 BCE. The Persian plan to tempt Alexander across the river and kill him in the melee almost succeeded, but the Persian line broke, and Alexander's victory was complete. Greek mercenaries employed by the Persian king Darius were largely massacred, but 2,000 survivors were sent back to Macedonia in chains.

This victory exposed western Asia Minor to the Macedonians, and most cities hastened to open their gates. The tyrants were expelled and (in contrast to Macedonian policy in Greece) democracies were installed. Alexander thus underlined his Panhellenic policy, already symbolized in the sending of 300 panoplies (sets of armour) taken at the Granicus as an offering dedicated to Athena at Athens by "Alexander son of Philip and the Greeks (except the Spartans) from the barbarians who inhabit Asia." (This formula, cited by the Greek historian Arrian in his history of Alexander's campaigns, is noteworthy for its omission of any reference to Macedonia.)

Yet the cities remained de facto under Alexander, and his appointment of Calas as satrap of Hellespontine Phrygia reflected his claim to succeed the Great King of Persia. When Miletus, encouraged by the proximity of the Persian fleet, resisted, Alexander took it by assault. Refusing a naval battle, he disbanded his own costly navy and announced that he would "defeat the Persian fleet on land," by occupying the coastal cities. In the region of Caria, the city of Halicarnassus resisted and was stormed. Ada, the widow and sister of the Caria satrap Idrieus, adopted Alexander as her son and, after expelling her brother Pixodarus, Alexander restored her to her satrapy. Some parts of Caria held out, however, until 332.

ASIA MINOR AND THE BATTLE OF ISSUS

In winter 334 BCE Alexander conquered western Asia Minor, subduing the hill tribes of Lycia and Pisidia. The following spring he advanced along the coastal road to Perga, passing the cliffs of Mt. Climax, thanks to a fortunate change of wind. The fall in the level of the sea was interpreted as a mark of divine favour by Alexander's flatterers, including the historian Callisthenes. At Gordium in Phrygia, tradition records his cutting of the Gordian knot, which could only be loosed by the man who was to rule Asia. This story, however, may be apocryphal or at least distorted.

At this point Alexander benefitted from the sudden death of Memnon, the competent Greek commander of the Persian fleet. From Gordium he pushed on to Ancyra (modern Ankara, Turkey) and thence south through Cappadocia and the Cilician Gates (modern Külek Boğazi). A fever held him up for a time in Cilicia. Meanwhile, Darius with his Grand Army had advanced northward on the eastern side of Mt. Amanus. Intelligence on both sides was faulty, and Alexander was already encamped by Myriandrus (near modern Iskenderun, Turkey) when he learned that Darius was astride his line of communications at Issus, north of Alexander's position in the autumn of 333. Turning, Alexander found Darius drawn up along the Pinarus River. In the battle that followed, Alexander won a decisive victory. The struggle turned into a Persian rout and Darius fled, leaving his family in Alexander's hands. It is reported that the women were treated with chivalrous care.

CONQUEST OF THE MEDITERRANEAN COAST AND EGYPT

From Issus Alexander marched south into Syria and Phoenicia, his object being to isolate the Persian fleet from its bases and so to destroy it as an effective fighting force. The Phoenician cities Marathus and Aradus came over quietly, and Parmenio was sent ahead to secure Damascus and its rich booty, including Darius's war chest. In reply to a letter from Darius offering peace, Alexander replied arrogantly, recapitulating the historic wrongs of Greece and demanding unconditional surrender to himself as lord of Asia. After taking Byblos (modern Jubayl) and Sidon (Arabic Ṣaydā), he met with a check at Tyre, where he was refused entry into the island city. He thereupon prepared to use all methods of siegecraft to take it, but the Tyrians resisted, holding out for seven months. In the meantime (winter 333–332) the Persians had counterattacked by land in Asia Minor—where they were defeated by Antigonus, the satrap of Greater Phrygia—and by sea, recapturing a number of cities and islands.

While the siege of Tyre was in progress, Darius sent a new offer: he would pay a huge ransom of 10,000 talents for his family and cede all his lands west of the Euphrates. "I would accept," Parmenio is reported to have said, "were I Alexander"; "I too," was the famous retort, "were I Parmenio." The storming of Tyre in July 332 was Alexander's greatest military achievement; it was attended with great carnage and the sale of the women and children into slavery. Leaving Parmenio in Syria, Alexander advanced south without opposition until he reached Gaza on its high mound; there bitter resistance halted him for two months, and he sustained a serious shoulder wound during a sortie. There is no basis for the tradition that he turned aside to visit Jerusalem.

In November 332 he reached Egypt. The people welcomed him as their deliverer, and the Persian satrap Mazaces wisely surrendered. At Memphis Alexander sacrificed to Apis, the Greek term for Hapi, the sacred Egyptian bull, and was crowned with the traditional double crown of the pharaohs; the native priests were placated and their religion encouraged. He spent the winter organizing Egypt, where he employed Egyptian governors, keeping the army under a separate Macedonian command. He founded the city of Alexandria near the western arm of the Nile River on a fine site between the sea and Lake Mareotis, protected by the island of Pharos, and had it laid out by the Rhodian architect Deinocrates. He is also said to have sent an expedition to discover the causes of the flooding of the Nile. From Alexandria he marched along the coast to Paraetonium and from there inland to visit the celebrated oracle of the god Amon (at Sīwah); the difficult journey was later embroidered with flattering legends. On his reaching the oracle in its oasis, the priest gave him the traditional salutation of a pharaoh, as son of Amon; Alexander consulted the god on the success of his expedition but revealed the reply to no one. Later the incident was to contribute to the story that he was the son of Zeus and, thus, to his "deification." In spring 331 he returned to Tyre, appointed a Macedonian satrap for Syria, and prepared to advance into Mesopotamia. His conquest of Egypt had completed his control of the whole eastern Mediterranean coast.

In July 331 Alexander was at Thapsacus on the Euphrates River. Instead of taking the direct route down the river to Babylon, he made across northern Mesopotamia toward the Tigris River, and Darius, learning of this move from an advance force sent under Mazaeus to the Euphrates crossing, marched up the Tigris to oppose him. The decisive battle of the war was fought on October 31, on the plain of Gaugamela between Nineveh and Arbela. Alexander pursued the defeated Persian forces for 35 miles (46 km) to Arbela, but Darius escaped with his Bactrian cavalry and Greek mercenaries into Media.

Alexander now occupied Babylon, city and province; Mazaeus, who surrendered it, was confirmed as satrap in conjunction with a Macedonian troop commander, and quite exceptionally was granted the right to coin. As in Egypt, the local priesthood was encouraged. Susa, the capital, also surrendered, releasing huge treasures amounting to 50,000 gold talents; here Alexander established Darius's family in comfort. Crushing the mountain tribe of the Ouxians, he now pressed on over the Zagros range into Persia proper and, successfully turning the Pass of the Persian Gates, held by the satrap Ariobarzanes, he entered the Persian capital Persepolis and its predecessor, Pasargadae. At Persepolis he ceremonially burned down the palace of Xerxes, as a symbol that the Panhellenic war of revenge was at an end; for such seems the probable significance of an act that tradition later explained as a drunken frolic inspired by Thaïs, an Athenian courtesan. In spring 330 Alexander marched north into Media and occupied its capital Ecbatana. The Thessalians and Greek allies were sent home; henceforward he was waging a purely personal war.

As Mazaeus's appointment indicated, Alexander's views on the empire were changing. He had come to envisage a joint ruling people consisting of Macedonians and Persians, and this served to augment the misunderstanding that now arose between him and his people. Before continuing his pursuit of Darius, who had retreated into Bactria, he assembled all the Persian treasure and entrusted it to Harpalus, who was to hold it at Ecbatana as chief treasurer. Parmenio was also left behind in Media to control communications; the presence of this older man had perhaps become irksome.

In midsummer 330 Alexander set out for the eastern provinces at a high speed via Rhagae (modern Rayy, near Tehrān) and the Caspian Gates, where he learned that Bessus, the satrap of Bactria, had deposed Darius. After a skirmish near modern Shāhrūd, the usurper had Darius stabbed and left him to die. Alexander sent his body for burial with due honours in the royal tombs at Persepolis.

CAMPAIGN EASTWARD, TO CENTRAL ASIA

Darius's death left no obstacle to Alexander's claim to be Great King, and a Rhodian inscription of this year (330) calls him "lord of Asia"—i.e., of the Persian empire; soon afterward his Asian coins carry the title of king. Crossing the Elburz Mountains to the Caspian Sea, he seized Zadracarta in Hyrcania and received the submission of a group of satraps and Persian notables, some of whom he confirmed in their offices; in a diversion westward, perhaps to modern Āmol, Iran, he reduced the Mardi, a mountain people who inhabited the Elburz Mountains. He also accepted the surrender of Darius's Greek mercenaries. His advance eastward was now rapid. In Aria he reduced Satibarzanes, who had offered submission only to revolt, and he founded Alexandria of the Arians (modern Herāt, Afghanistan). At Phrada in Drangiana (either near modern Nad-e 'Ali in the Sīstān region or farther north at Farāh, Afghanistan), he at last took steps to destroy Parmenio and his family. Philotas, Parmenio's son, commander of the elite Companion cavalry, was implicated in an alleged plot against Alexander's life, condemned by the army, and executed; and a secret message was sent to Cleander, Parmenio's second in command, who obediently assassinated him. This ruthless action excited widespread horror but strengthened Alexander's position relative to his critics and those whom he regarded as his father's men. All Parmenio's adherents were now eliminated and men close to Alexander promoted. The Companion cavalry was reorganized in two sections, each containing four squadrons (now known as hipparchies); one group was commanded by Alexander's oldest friend, Hephaestion, the other by Cleitus, an older man. From Phrada, Alexander pressed on during the winter of 330–329 up the valley of the Helmand River, through Arachosia, and over the mountains past the site of modern Kabul, Afghanistan, into the country of the Paropamisadae, where he founded Alexandria by the Caucasus Mountains.

Bessus was now in Bactria raising a national revolt in the eastern satrapies with the usurped title of Great King. Crossing the Hindu Kush range northward over the Khawak Pass (11,650 feet [3,550 metres]), Alexander brought his army, despite food shortages, to Drapsaca (sometimes identified with modern Banu [Andarab], probably farther north at Qunduz); outflanked, Bessus fled beyond the Oxus River (modern Amu Darya), and Alexander, marching west to Bactra (modern Balkh [Vazī rābād] in Afghanistan), appointed loyal satraps in Bactria and Aria. Crossing the Oxus, he sent his general Ptolemy in pursuit of Bessus, who had meanwhile been overthrown by the Sogdian Spitamenes. Bessus was captured, flogged, and sent to Bactra, where he was later mutilated after the Persian manner (losing his nose and ears); in due course he was publicly executed at Ecbatana.

From Maracanda (modern Samarkand, Uzbekistan) Alexander advanced by way of Cyropolis to the Jaxartes River (modern Syr Darya), the eastern boundary of the Persian empire. There he broke the opposition of the Scythian nomads by his use of catapults and, after defeating them in a battle on the north bank of the river, pursued them into the interior. On the site of modern Khujand, Tajikistan, on the Jaxartes, he founded a city, Alexandria Eschate, "the farthest." Meanwhile, Spitamenes had raised all Sogdiana in revolt behind him, bringing in the Massagetai, a people of the Shaka confederacy. It took Alexander until the autumn of 328 to crush this opponent, the most determined he had encountered in his campaigns. Later in the same year he attacked Oxyartes and the remaining barons who held out in the hills of Paraetacene (modern Tajikistan); volunteers seized the crag on which Oxyartes had his stronghold, and among the captives was his daughter, Roxana. In reconciliation Alexander married her, and the rest of his opponents were either won over or crushed.

An incident that occurred at Maracanda widened the breach between Alexander and many of his Macedonians. He murdered Cleitus, one of his most trusted commanders, in a drunken quarrel; but his excessive display of remorse led the army to pass a decree convicting Cleitus posthumously of treason. The event marked a step in Alexander's progress toward Eastern absolutism, and this growing attitude found its outward expression in his use of Persian royal dress. Shortly afterward, at Bactra, he attempted to impose the Persian court ceremonial, involving prostration (proskynesis), on the Greeks and Macedonians too; but to them this custom, habitual for Persians entering the king's presence, implied an act of worship and was intolerable before a man. Even Callisthenes, historian and nephew of Aristotle, whose ostentatious flattery had perhaps encouraged Alexander to see himself in the role of a god, refused to abase himself. Macedonian laughter caused the experiment to founder, and Alexander abandoned it. Shortly afterward, however, Callisthenes was held to be privy to a conspiracy among the royal pages and was executed (or died in prison; accounts vary); resentment of this action alienated sympathy from Alexander within the Peripatetic school of philosophers, with which Callisthenes had close connections.

INVASION OF INDIA

In early summer 327 BCE Alexander left Bactria with a reinforced army under a reorganized command. If Plutarch's figure of 120,000 men has any reality, however, it must include all kinds of auxiliary services, together with muleteers, camel drivers, medical corps, peddlers, entertainers, women, and children; the fighting strength perhaps stood at about 35,000. Recrossing the Hindu Kush, probably by Bamiyan and the Ghorband Valley, Alexander divided his forces. Half the army with the baggage under Hephaestion and Perdiccas, both cavalry commanders, was sent through the Khyber Pass, while he himself led the rest, together with his siege train, through the hills to the north. His advance through Swat and Gandhara was marked by the storming of the almost impregnable pinnacle of Aornos, the modern Pir-Sar in Pakistan, a few miles west of the Indus River and north of the Buner River, an impressive feat of siegecraft. In spring 326, crossing the Indus near Attock, Alexander entered Taxila, whose ruler, Taxiles, furnished elephants and troops in return for aid against his rival Porus, who ruled the lands between the Hydaspes (modern Jhelum) and the Acesines (modern Chenab) rivers. In June Alexander fought his last great battle on the left bank of the Hydaspes. He founded two cities there, Alexandria Nicaea (to celebrate his victory) and Bucephala (named after his horse Bucephalus, which died there); and Porus became his ally.

How much Alexander knew of India beyond the Hyphasis (probably the modern Beas River) is uncertain; there is no conclusive proof that he had heard of the Ganges River. But he was anxious to press on farther, and he had advanced to the Hyphasis when his army mutinied, refusing to go farther in the tropical rain; they were weary in body and spirit, and Coenus, one of Alexander's four chief marshals, acted as their spokesman. On finding the army adamant, Alexander agreed to turn back.

On the Hyphasis he erected 12 altars to the 12 Olympian gods, and on the Hydaspes he built a fleet of 800 to 1,000 ships. Leaving Porus, he then proceeded down the river and into the Indus, with half his forces on shipboard and half marching in three columns down the two banks. The fleet was commanded by Nearchus, and Alexander's own captain was Onesicritus; both later wrote accounts of the campaign. The march was attended with much fighting and heavy, pitiless slaughter; at the storming of one town of the Malli near the Hydraotes (Ravi) River, Alexander received a severe wound which left him weakened.

On reaching Patala, located at the head of the Indus delta, he built a harbour and docks and explored both arms of the Indus, which probably then ran into the Rann of Kachchh (Kutch). He planned to lead part of his forces back by land, while the rest in perhaps 100 to 150 ships under the command of Nearchus, a Cretan with naval experience, made a voyage of exploration along the Persian Gulf. Local opposition led Nearchus to set sail in September (325), and he was held up for three weeks until he could pick up the northeast monsoon in late October. In September Alexander too set out along the coast through Gedrosia (modern Baluchistan), but he was soon compelled by mountainous country to turn inland, thus failing in his project to establish food depots for the fleet. Craterus, a high-ranking officer, already had been sent off with the baggage and siege train, the elephants, and the sick and wounded, together with three battalions of the phalanx, by way of the Mulla Pass, Quetta, and Kandahar into the Helmand Valley; from there he was to march through Drangiana to rejoin the main army on the Amanis (modern Minab) River in Carmania. Alexander's march through Gedrosia proved disastrous; waterless desert and shortage of food and fuel caused great suffering, and many, especially women and children, perished in a sudden monsoon flood while encamped in a wadi. At length, at the Amanis, he was rejoined by Nearchus and the fleet, which also had suffered losses.

CONSOLIDATION OF THE EMPIRE

Alexander now proceeded farther with the policy of replacing senior officials and executing defaulting governors on which he had already embarked before leaving India. Between 326 and 324 over a third of his satraps were superseded and six were put to death, including the Persian satraps of Persis, Susiana, Carmania, and Paraetacene; three generals in Media, including Cleander, the brother of Coenus (who had died a little earlier), were accused of extortion and summoned to Carmania, where they were arrested, tried, and executed. How far the rigour that from now onward Alexander displayed against his governors represents exemplary punishment for gross maladministration during his absence and how far the elimination of men he had come to distrust (as in the case of Philotas and

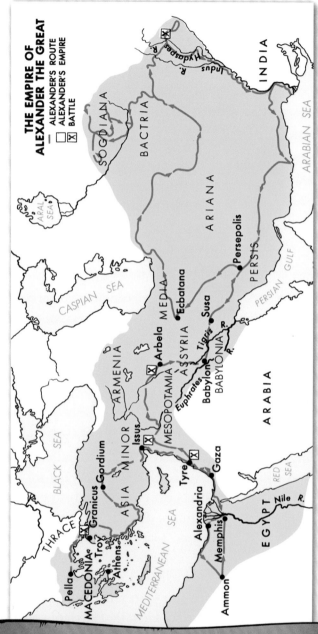

Alexander the Great's conquests freed the West from Persian rule and spread Greek civilization and culture into Asia and Egypt. His vast empire stretched east into India.

Parmenio) is debatable; but the ancient sources generally favourable to him comment adversely on his severity.

In spring 324 he was back in Susa, capital of Elam and administrative centre of the Persian Empire; the story of his journey through Carmania in a drunken revel, dressed as Dionysus, is embroidered, if not wholly apocryphal. He found that his treasurer, Harpalus, evidently fearing punishment for peculation, had absconded with 6,000 mercenaries and 5,000 talents to Greece; arrested in Athens, he escaped and later was murdered in Crete. At Susa Alexander held a feast to celebrate the seizure of the Persian Empire, at which, in furtherance of his policy of fusing Macedonians and Persians into one master race, he and 80 of his officers took Persian wives; he and Hephaestion married Darius's daughters Barsine (also called Stateira) and Drypetis, respectively, and 10,000 of his soldiers with native wives were given generous dowries.

This policy of racial fusion brought increasing friction to Alexander's relations with his Macedonians, who had no sympathy for his changed concept of the empire. His determination to incorporate Persians on equal terms in the army and the administration of the provinces was bitterly resented. This discontent was now fanned by the arrival of 30,000 native youths who had received a Macedonian military training and by the introduction of Asians from Bactria, Sogdiana, Arachosia, and other parts of the empire into the Companion cavalry; whether Asians had previously served with the Companions is uncertain, but if so they must have formed separate squadrons. In addition, Persian nobles had been accepted into the royal cavalry bodyguard. Peucestas, the new governor of Persis, gave this policy full support to flatter Alexander; but most Macedonians saw it as a threat to their own privileged position.

The issue came to a head at Opis (324), when Alexander's decision to send home Macedonian veterans under Craterus was interpreted as a move toward transferring the seat of power to Asia. There was an open mutiny involving all but the royal bodyguard; but when Alexander dismissed his whole army and enrolled Persians instead, the opposition broke down. An emotional scene of reconciliation was followed by a vast banquet with 9,000 guests to celebrate the ending of the misunderstanding and the partnership in government of Macedonians and Persians—but not, as has been argued, the incorporation of all the subject peoples as partners in the commonwealth. Ten thousand veterans were now sent back to Macedonia with gifts, and the crisis was surmounted.

In summer 324 Alexander attempted to solve another problem, that of the wandering mercenaries, of whom there were thousands in Asia and Greece, many of them political exiles from their own cities. A decree brought by Nicanor to Europe and proclaimed at Olympia (September 324) required the Greek cities of the Greek League to receive back all exiles and their families (except the Thebans), a measure that implied some modification of the oligarchic regimes maintained in the Greek cities by Alexander's governor Antipater. Alexander now planned to recall Antipater and supersede him by Craterus; but he was to die before this could be done.

In autumn 324 Hephaestion died in Ecbatana, and Alexander indulged in extravagant mourning for his closest friend; he was given a royal funeral in Babylon with a pyre costing 10,000 talents. His post of chiliarch (grand vizier) was left unfilled. It was probably in connection with a general order now sent out to the Greeks to honour Hephaestion as a hero that Alexander linked the demand that he himself should be accorded divine honours. For a long time his mind had dwelt on ideas of godhead. Greek thought drew no very decided line of demarcation between god and man, for legend offered more than one example of men who, by their achievements, acquired divine status. Alexander had on several occasions encouraged favourable comparison of his own accomplishments with those of Dionysus or Heracles. He now seems to have become convinced of the reality of his own divinity and to have required its acceptance by others. There is no reason to assume that his demand had any political background (divine status gave its possessor no particular rights in a Greek city); it was rather a symptom of growing megalomania and emotional instability. The cities perforce complied, but often ironically: the Spartan decree read, "Since Alexander wishes to be a god, let him be a god."

In the winter of 324 Alexander carried out a savage punitive expedition against the Cossaeans in the hills of Luristan. The following spring at Babylon he received complimentary embassies from the Libyans and from the Bruttians, Etruscans, and Lucanians of Italy; but the story that embassies also came from more distant peoples, such as Carthaginians, Celts, Iberians, and even Romans, is a later invention. Representatives of the cities of Greece also came, garlanded as befitted Alexander's divine status. Following up Nearchus's voyage, he now founded an Alexandria at the mouth of the Tigris and made plans to develop sea communications with India, for which an expedition along the Arabian coast was to be a preliminary. He also dispatched Heracleides, an officer, to explore the Hyrcanian (i.e., Caspian) Sea. Suddenly, in Babylon, while busy with plans to improve the irrigation of the Euphrates and to settle the coast of the Persian Gulf, Alexander was taken ill after a prolonged banquet and drinking bout; 10 days later, on June 13, 323, he died in his 33rd year; he had reigned for 12 years and eight months. His body, diverted to Egypt by Ptolemy, the later king, was eventually placed in a golden coffin in Alexandria. Both in Egypt and elsewhere in the Greek cities he received divine honours.

No heir had been appointed to the throne, and his generals adopted Philip II's half-witted illegitimate son, Philip Arrhidaeus, and Alexander's posthumous son by Roxana, Alexander IV, as kings, sharing out the satrapies among themselves, after much bargaining. The empire could hardly survive Alexander's death as a unit. Both kings were murdered, Arrhidaeus in 317 and Alexander in 310/309. The provinces became independent kingdoms, and the generals, following Antigonus's lead in 306, took the title of king.

NEARCHUS

(d. probably 312 BCE)

Nearchus was an officer in the Macedonian army under Alexander the Great who, on Alexander's orders, sailed from the Hydaspes River in western India to the Persian Gulf and up the Euphrates River to Babylon. Earlier, in 333, Alexander had made Nearchus satrap (provincial governor) of the newly conquered Lycia and Pamphylia in Asia Minor (Anatolia). Nearchus embarked on his expedition in 325, when Alexander descended the Indus River to the sea.

Nearchus chronicled the journey in a detailed narrative, a full abstract of which is included in Arrian's *Indica* (2nd century CE). Nearchus was unable to play any significant role in the struggles following Alexander's death (323); the statement of a late source that he recovered his former satrapies is doubtful.

PYTHEAS

(fl. 300 BCE, Massalia, Gaul)

The navigator, geographer, and astronomer Pytheas was the first Greek to visit and describe the British Isles and the Atlantic coast of Europe. Though his principal work, *On the Ocean*, is lost, something is known of his ventures through the Greek historian Polybius (*c.* 200–*c.* 118 BCE).

Sailing from the Mediterranean Sea into the Atlantic, Pytheas stopped at the Phoenician city of Gades (present-day Cádiz, Spain), probably followed the European shoreline to the tip of Brittany, and eventually reached Belerium (Land's End, Cornwall), where he visited the tin mines, famous in the ancient world. He claimed to have explored a large part of Britain on foot; he accurately estimated its circumference at 4,000 miles (6,400 km). He also estimated the distance from north Britain to Massalia (Marseille) at 1,050 miles (1,690 km); the actual distance is 1,120 miles (1,800 km). He visited some northern European countries and may have reached the mouth of the Vistula River on the Baltic Sea. He also told of Thule, the northernmost inhabited island, six days' sail from northern Britain and extending at least to the Arctic Circle; the region he visited may have been Iceland or Norway.

His comments on small points—e.g., on the native drinks made of cereals and honey and the use of threshing barns (contrasted with open-air threshing in Mediterranean regions)—show acute observation. His scientific interests appear from his calculations made

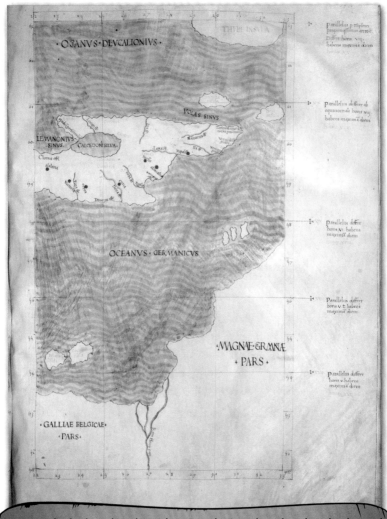

Map of Thule Island in the South Sandwich Islands, based on details attributed to the Greek navigator Pytheas. DEA Picture Library/Getty Images

with a sundial at the summer solstice and from notes on the lengthening days as he traveled northward. He also observed that the polestar is not at the true pole and that the Moon affects tides.

ZHANG QIAN

(b. Chenggu [now in Shaanxi province],
China—d. 114 BCE)

The Chinese explorer Zhang Qian (or Chang Ch'ien)
was the first man to bring back a reliable account

A statue of the ancient explorer Zhang Qian acting as a sentinel outside a museum in Gansu, China. © JTB Photo/SuperStock

of the lands of Central Asia to the court of China. He was dispatched by the Han dynasty emperor Wudi in 138 BCE to establish relations with the Yuezhi people, a Central Asian tribal group that spoke an Indo-European language. Captured by the Xiongnu, nomadic enemies of China, he was detained for 10 years. Nevertheless, he managed to reach his destination and returned to China after an absence of 13 years.

Seven years later he was sent on another mission, this time to the Wusun, another Indo-European people living in the Ili River valley north of the Tarim Basin. In addition to traveling himself, he sent his assistant to visit the Fergana Valley (Uzbekistan), Bactria (Afghanistan), and Sogdiana (west Turkestan, now in Uzbekistan). He gathered information on Parthia, India, and other states in the area. His mission brought the Chinese into contact with the outposts of Hellenistic culture established by Alexander the Great, opened the way for exchanges of envoys between these Central Asian states and the Han, and led to the introduction into China of a superior breed of horses and new plants, such as grapes and alfalfa.

JULIUS CAESAR

(b. July 12/13, 100? BCE, Rome [Italy]—d. March
15, 44 BCE, Rome)

The celebrated Roman general and statesman Gaius
Julius Caesar was the conqueror of Gaul (58–50 BCE),
victor in the Civil War of 49–45 BCE, and dictator (46–44
BCE) of Rome. He was launching a series of political and
social reforms when he was assassinated by a group of
nobles in the Senate House on the Ides of March. Caesar
changed the course of the history of the Greco-Roman
world decisively and irreversibly. Although Caesar's subjugation of Gaul was not perceived by him nor by later
historians to be his most important achievement, it
still was of great significance in its scope and audacity
and was a continuation of the Alexandrian tradition of the
conqueror-adventurer.

The Greco-Roman society has been extinct for so
long that most of the names of its great men mean little
to the average, educated modern person. But Caesar's
name, like Alexander's, is still on people's lips throughout
the Christian and Islamic worlds. Even people who know
nothing of Caesar as a historic personality are familiar
with his family name as a title signifying a ruler who is in
some sense uniquely supreme or paramount—the meaning of Kaiser in German, tsar in the Slavonic languages,
and qayṣar in the languages of the Islamic world.

Caesar's gens (clan) name, Julius (Iulius), is also familiar
in the Christian world; for in Caesar's lifetime the Roman

EXPLORERS OF ANTIQUITY: FROM ALEXANDER THE GREAT TO MARCO POLO

month Quintilis, in which he was born, was renamed "July" in his honour. This name has survived, as has Caesar's reform of the calendar. The old Roman calendar was inaccurate and manipulated for political purposes. Caesar's calendar, the Julian calendar, is still partially in force in the Eastern Orthodox Christian countries; and the Gregorian calendar, now in use in the West, is the Julian, slightly corrected by Pope Gregory XIII.

FAMILY BACKGROUND AND CAREER

Caesar's gens, the Julii, were patricians—i.e., members of Rome's original aristocracy, which had coalesced in the 4th century BCE with a number of leading plebeian (commoner) families to form the nobility that had been the governing class in Rome since then. By Caesar's time, the number of surviving patrician gentes was small; and in the gens Julia the Caesares seem to have been the only surviving family. Though some of the most powerful noble families were patrician, patrician blood was no longer a political advantage; it was actually a handicap, since a patrician was debarred from holding the paraconstitutional but powerful office of tribune of the plebs. The Julii Caesares traced their lineage back to the goddess Venus, but the family was not snobbish or conservative-minded. It was also not rich or influential or even distinguished.

A Roman noble won distinction for himself and his family by securing election to a series of public offices, which culminated in the consulship, with the censorship possibly to follow. This was a difficult task for even the ablest and most gifted noble unless he was backed by substantial family wealth and influence. Rome's victory over Carthage in the Second Punic War (218–201 BCE) had made Rome the paramount power in the Mediterranean basin; an influential Roman noble family's clients (that is, protégés who, in return, gave their patrons their political support) might include kings and even whole nations, besides numerous private individuals. The requirements and the costs of a Roman political career in Caesar's day were high, and the competition was severe; but the potential profits were of enormous magnitude. One of the perquisites of the praetorship and the consulship was the government of a province, which gave ample opportunity for plunder. The whole Mediterranean world was, in fact, at the mercy of the Roman nobility and of a new class of Roman businessmen, the equites ("knights"), which had grown rich on military contracts and on tax farming.

Military manpower was supplied by the Roman peasantry. This class had been partly dispossessed by an economic revolution following on the devastation caused by the Second Punic War. The Roman governing class had consequently come to be hated and discredited at home and abroad. From 133 BCE onward there had been a series of alternate revolutionary and counter-revolutionary paroxysms. It was evident that the misgovernment of the Roman state and the Greco-Roman world by the Roman nobility could not continue indefinitely and it was fairly clear that the most probable alternative was some form of military dictatorship backed by dispossessed Italian peasants who had turned to long-term military service.

The traditional competition among members of the Roman nobility for office and the spoils of office was thus threatening to turn into a desperate race for seizing autocratic power. The Julii Caesares did not seem to be in the running. It was true that Sextus Caesar, who was perhaps the dictator's uncle, had been one of the consuls for 91 BCE, and Lucius Caesar, one of the consuls for 90 BCE, was a distant cousin, whose son and namesake was consul for 64

BCE. In 90, Rome's Italian allies had seceded from Rome because of the Roman government's obstinate refusal to grant them Roman citizenship, and, as consul, Lucius Caesar had introduced emergency legislation for granting citizenship to the citizens of all Italian ally states that had not taken up arms or that had returned to their allegiance.

Whoever had been consul in this critical year would have had to initiate such legislation, whatever his personal political predilections. There is evidence, however, that the Julii Caesares, though patricians, had already committed themselves to the antinobility party. An aunt of the future dictator had married Gaius Marius, a self-made man (*novus homo*) who had forced his way up to the summit by his military ability and had made the momentous innovation of recruiting his armies from the dispossessed peasants.

The date of Caesar the dictator's birth has long been disputed. The day was July 12 or 13; the traditional (and perhaps most probable) year is 100 BCE; but if this date is correct, Caesar must have held each of his offices two years in advance of the legal minimum age. His father, Gaius Caesar, died when Caesar was but 16; his mother, Aurelia, was a notable woman, and it seems certain that he owed much to her.

In spite of the inadequacy of his resources, Caesar seems to have chosen a political career as a matter of course. From the beginning, he probably privately aimed at winning office, not just for the sake of the honours but in order to achieve the power to put the misgoverned Roman state and Greco-Roman world into better order in accordance with ideas of his own. It is improbable that Caesar deliberately sought monarchical power until after he had crossed the Rubicon in 49 BCE, though sufficient power to impose his will, as he was determined to do, proved to mean monarchical power.

In 84 BCE Caesar committed himself publicly to the radical side by marrying Cornelia, a daughter of Lucius Cornelius Cinna, a noble who was Marius' associate in revolution. In 83 Lucius Cornelius Sulla returned to Italy from the East and led the successful counter-revolution of 83–82; Sulla then ordered Caesar to divorce Cornelia. Caesar refused and came close to losing not only his property (such as it was) but his life as well. He found it advisable to remove himself from Italy and to do military service, first in the province of Asia and then in Cilicia.

In 78 BCE, after Sulla's death, he returned to Rome and started on his political career in the conventional way, by acting as a prosecuting advocate—of course, in his case, against prominent Sullan counter-revolutionaries. His first target, Gnaeus Cornelius Dolabella, was defended by Quintus Hortensius, the leading advocate of the day, and was acquitted by the extortion-court jury, composed exclusively of senators.

Caesar then went to Rhodes to study oratory under a famous professor, Molon. En route he was captured by pirates (one of the symptoms of the anarchy into which the Roman nobility had allowed the Mediterranean world to fall). Caesar raised his ransom, raised a naval force, captured his captors, and had them crucified—all this as a private individual holding no public office. In 74, when Mithradates VI Eupator, king of Pontus, renewed war on the Romans, Caesar raised a private army to combat him.

In his absence from Rome, Caesar was made a member of the politico-ecclesiastical college of pontifices; and on his return he gained one of the elective military tribune-ships. Caesar now worked to undo the Sullan constitution in cooperation with Pompey (Gnaeus Pompeius), who had started his career as a lieutenant of Sulla but had changed sides since Sulla's death. In 69 or 68 BCE Caesar was elected quaestor (the first rung on the Roman political ladder). In the same year his wife, Cornelia, and his aunt Julia, Marius' widow, died; in public funeral orations in their honour, Caesar found opportunities for praising Cinna and Marius. Caesar afterward married Pompeia, a distant relative of Pompey. Caesar served his quaestorship in the province of Farther Spain (modern Andalusia and Portugal).

Caesar was elected one of the curule aediles for 65 BCE, and he celebrated his tenure of this office by unusually lavish expenditure with borrowed money. He was elected pontifex maximus in 63 by a political dodge. By now he had become a controversial political figure. After the suppression of Catiline's conspiracy in 63, Caesar, as well as the millionaire Marcus Licinius Crassus, was accused of complicity. It seems unlikely that either of them had committed himself to Catiline; but Caesar proposed in the Senate a more merciful alternative to the death penalty, which the consul Cicero was asking for the arrested conspirators. In the uproar in the Senate, Caesar's motion was defeated.

Caesar was elected a praetor for 62 BCE. Toward the end of the year of his praetorship, a scandal was caused by Publius Clodius in Caesar's house at the celebration there of the rites, for women only, of Bona Dea (a Roman deity of fruitfulness, both in the Earth and in women). Caesar consequently divorced Pompeia. He obtained the governorship of Farther Spain for 61–60. His creditors did not let him leave Rome until Crassus had gone bail for a quarter of his debts; but a military expedition beyond the northwest frontier of his province enabled Caesar to win loot for himself as well as for his soldiers, with a balance left over for the treasury. This partial financial recovery enabled him, after his return to Rome in 60, to stand for the consulship for 59.

THE FIRST TRIUMVIRATE AND THE CONQUEST OF GAUL

The value of the consulship lay in the lucrative provincial governorship to which it would normally lead. On the eve of the consular elections for 59 BCE, the Senate sought to allot to the two future consuls for 59, as their proconsular provinces, the unprofitable supervision of forests and cattle trails in Italy. The Senate also secured by massive bribery the election of an anti-Caesarean, Marcus Calpurnius Bibulus. But they failed to prevent Caesar's election as the other consul.

Caesar now succeeded in organizing an irresistible coalition of political bosses. Pompey had carried out his mission to put the East in order with notable success, but after his return to Italy and his disbandment of his army in 62, the Senate had thwarted him—particularly by preventing him from securing land allotments for his veterans. Caesar, who had assiduously cultivated Pompey's friendship, now entered into a secret pact with him. Caesar's master stroke was to persuade Crassus to join the partnership, the so-called first triumvirate. Crassus—like Pompey, a former lieutenant of Sulla—had been one of the most active of Pompey's obstructors so far. Only Caesar, on good terms with both, was in a position to reconcile them. Early in 59, Pompey sealed his alliance with Caesar by marrying Caesar's only child, Julia. Caesar married Calpurnia, daughter of Lucius Piso, who became consul in 58.

As consul, Caesar introduced a bill for the allotment of Roman public lands in Italy, on which the first charge was to be a provision for Pompey's soldiers. The bill was vetoed by three tribunes of the plebs, and Caesar's colleague Bibulus announced his intention of preventing the

Marble statue of Julius Caesar. © Dariusz Kopestynski/Fotolia

transaction of public business by watching the skies for portents whenever the public assembly was convened. Caesar then cowed the opposition by employing some of Pompey's veterans to make a riot, and the distribution was carried out. Pompey's settlement of the East was ratified *en bloc* by an act negotiated by an agent of Caesar, the tribune of the plebs Publius Vatinius. Caesar himself initiated a noncontroversial and much-needed act for punishing misconduct by governors of provinces.

Another act negotiated by Vatinius gave Caesar Cisalpine Gaul (between the Alps, the Apennines, and the Adriatic) and Illyricum. His tenure was to last until February 28, 54 BCE. When the governor-designate of Transalpine Gaul suddenly died, this province, also, was assigned to Caesar at Pompey's instance. Cisalpine Gaul gave Caesar a military recruiting ground; Transalpine Gaul gave him a springboard for conquests beyond Rome's northwest frontier.

Between 58 and 50 BCE, Caesar conquered the rest of Gaul up to the left bank of the Rhine and subjugated it so effectively that it remained passive under Roman rule throughout the Roman civil wars between 49 and 31. This achievement was all the more amazing in light of the fact that the Romans did not possess any great superiority in military equipment over their northern European foes. Indeed, the Gallic cavalry was probably superior to the Roman, horseman for horseman. Rome's military superiority lay in its mastery of strategy, tactics, discipline, and military engineering. In Gaul, Rome also had the advantage of being able to deal separately with dozens of relatively small, independent, and uncooperative states. Caesar conquered these piecemeal, and the concerted attempt made by a number of them in 52 to shake off the Roman yoke came too late.

Great though this achievement was, its relative importance in Caesar's career and in Roman history has been overestimated in Western tradition (as have his brief raids on Britain). In Caesar's mind his conquest of Gaul was probably carried out only as a means to his ultimate end. He was acquiring the military manpower, the plunder, and the prestige that he needed to secure a free hand for the prosecution of the task of reorganizing the Roman state and the rest of the Greco-Roman world. This final achievement of Caesar's looms much larger than his conquest of Gaul, when it is viewed in the wider setting of world history and not just in the narrower setting of the Greco-Roman civilization's present daughter civilization in the West.

In 58 BCE Rome's northwestern frontier, established in 125 BCE, ran from the Alps down the left bank of the upper Rhône River to the Pyrenees, skirting the southeastern foot of the Cévennes and including the upper basin of the Garonne River without reaching the Gallic shore of the Atlantic. In 58 Caesar intervened beyond this line, first to drive back the Helvetii, who had been migrating westward from their home in what is now central Switzerland. He then crushed Ariovistus, a German soldier of fortune from beyond the Rhine. In 57 Caesar subdued the distant and warlike Belgic group of Gallic peoples in the north, while his lieutenant Publius Licinius Crassus subdued what are now the regions of Normandy and Brittany.

In 56 the Veneti, in what is now southern Brittany, started a revolt in the northwest that was supported by the still unconquered Morini on the Gallic coast of the Straits of Dover and the Menapii along the south bank of the lower Rhine. Caesar reconquered the Veneti with some difficulty and treated them barbarously. He could not finish off the conquest of the Morini and Menapii before the end of the campaigning season of 56 BCE, and in the winter of 56–55 the Menapii were temporarily expelled from their home by two immigrant German peoples, the

Usipetes and Tencteri. These peoples were exterminated by Caesar in 55. In the same year he bridged the Rhine just below modern Koblenz to raid Germany on the other side of the river, and then crossed the Channel to raid Britain. In 54 he raided Britain again and subdued a serious revolt in northeastern Gaul. In 53 he subdued further revolts in Gaul and bridged the Rhine again for a second raid.

The crisis of Caesar's Gallic war came in 52 BCE. The peoples of central Gaul found a national leader in the Arvernian Vercingetorix. They planned to cut off the Roman forces from Caesar, who had been wintering on the other side of the Alps. They even attempted to invade the western end of the old Roman province of Transalpine Gaul. Vercingetorix wanted to avoid pitched battles and sieges and to defeat the Romans by cutting off their supplies—partly by cavalry operations and partly by "scorched earth"—but he could not persuade his countrymen to adopt this painful policy wholeheartedly.

The Bituriges insisted on standing siege in their town Avaricum (Bourges), and Vercingetorix was unable to save it from being taken by storm within one month. Caesar then besieged Vercingetorix in Gergovia near modern Clermont-Ferrand. A Roman attempt to storm Gergovia was repulsed and resulted in heavy Roman losses—the first outright defeat that Caesar had suffered in Gaul. Caesar then defeated an attack on the Roman army on the march and was thus able to besiege Vercingetorix in Alesia, to the northwest of Dijon. Alesia, like Gergovia, was a position of great natural strength, and a large Gallic army came to relieve it; but this army was repulsed and dispersed by Caesar, and Vercingetorix then capitulated.

During the winter of 52–51 BCE and the campaigning season of 51, Caesar crushed a number of sporadic further revolts. The most determined of these rebels were the Bellovaci, between the Seine and Somme rivers, around modern Beauvais. Another rebel force stood siege in the south in the natural fortress of Uxellodunum (perhaps the Puy d'Issolu on the Dordogne) until its water supply gave out. Caesar had the survivors' hands cut off. He spent the year 50 in organizing the newly conquered territory. After that, he was ready to settle his accounts with his opponents at home.

ANTECEDENTS AND OUTCOME OF THE CIVIL WAR OF 49–45 BCE

During his conquest of Gaul, Caesar had been equally busy in preserving and improving his position at home. He used part of his growing wealth from Gallic loot to hire political agents in Rome.

Meanwhile the cohesion of the triumvirate had been placed under strain. Pompey had soon become restive toward his alarmingly successful ally Caesar, as had Crassus toward his old enemy Pompey. The alliance was patched up in April 56 BCE at a conference at Luca (Lucca), just inside Caesar's province of Cisalpine Gaul. It was arranged that Pompey and Crassus were to be the consuls for 55 and were to get laws promulgated prolonging Caesar's provincial commands for another five years and giving Crassus a five-year term in Syria and Pompey a five-year term in Spain. These laws were duly passed. Crassus was then eliminated by an annihilating defeat at the Parthians' hands in 53. The marriage link between Pompey and Caesar had been broken by Julia's death in 54. After this, Pompey irresolutely veered further and further away from Caesar, until, when the breach finally came, Pompey found himself committed to the nobility's side, though he and the nobility never trusted each other.

The issue was whether there should or should not be an interval between the date at which Caesar was to resign his provincial governorships and, therewith, the command over his armies and the date at which he would enter his proposed second consulship. If there were to be an interval, Caesar would be a private person during that time, vulnerable to attack by his enemies; if prosecuted and convicted, he would be ruined politically and might possibly lose his life. Caesar had to make sure that, until his entry on his second consulship, he should continue to hold at least one province with the military force to guarantee his security.

This issue had already been the object of a series of political maneuvers and countermaneuvers at Rome. The dates on which the issue turned are all in doubt. As had been agreed at Luca in 56 BCE, Caesar's commands had been prolonged for five years, apparently until February 28, 49, but this is not certain. In 52, a year in which Pompey was elected sole consul and given a five-year provincial command in Spain, Caesar was allowed by a law sponsored by all 10 tribunes to stand for the consulship in absentia. If he were to stand in 49 for the consulship for 48, he would be out of office, and therefore in danger, during the last 10 months of 49. As a safeguard for Caesar against this, there seems to have been an understanding—possibly a private one at Luca in 56 between him and Pompey—that the question of a successor to Caesar in his commands should not be raised in the Senate before March 1, 50. This maneuver would have ensured that Caesar would retain his commands until the end of 49. However, the question of replacing Caesar was actually raised in the Senate a number of times from 51 onward; each time Caesar had the dangerous proposals vetoed by tribunes of the plebs who were his agents—particularly Gaius Scribonius Curio in 50 and Mark Antony in 49.

The issue was brought to a head by one of the consuls for 50 BCE, Gaius Claudius Marcellus. He obtained resolutions from the Senate that Caesar should lay down his command (presumably at its terminal date) but that Pompey should not lay down his command simultaneously. Curio then obtained on December 1, 50, a resolution (by 370 votes to 22) that both men should lay down their commands simultaneously. Next day Marcellus (without authorization from the Senate) offered the command over all troops in Italy to Pompey, together with the power to raise more; and Pompey accepted. On January 1, 49, the Senate received from Caesar a proposal that he and Pompey should lay down their commands simultaneously. Caesar's message was peremptory, and the Senate resolved that Caesar should be treated as a public enemy if he did not lay down his command "by a date to be fixed."

On January 10–11, 49 BCE, Caesar led his troops across the little river Rubicon, the boundary between his province of Cisalpine Gaul and Italy proper. He thus committed the first act of war. This was not, however, the heart of the matter. The actual question of substance was whether the misgovernment of the Greco-Roman world by the Roman nobility should be allowed to continue or whether it should be replaced by an autocratic regime. Either alternative would result in a disastrous civil war. The subsequent partial recuperation of the Greco-Roman world under the principate suggests, however, that Caesarism was the lesser evil.

The civil war was a tragedy, for war was not wanted either by Caesar or by Pompey or even by a considerable part of the nobility, while the bulk of the Roman citizen body ardently hoped for the preservation of peace. By this time, however, the three parties that counted politically were all entrapped. Caesar's success in building up his political power had made the champions of the old regime so implacably hostile to him that he was now faced with a choice between putting himself at his enemies' mercy or seizing the monopoly of power at which he was accused of aiming. He found that he could not extricate himself from this dilemma by reducing his demands, as he eventually did, to the absolute minimum required for his security. As for Pompey, his growing jealousy of Caesar had led him so far toward the nobility that he could not come to terms with Caesar again without loss of face.

The first bout of the civil war moved swiftly. In 49 BCE Caesar drove his opponents out of Italy to the eastern side of the Straits of Otranto. He then crushed Pompey's army in Spain. Toward the end of 49, he followed Pompey across the Adriatic and retrieved a reverse at Dyrrachium by winning a decisive victory at Pharsalus on August 9, 48. Caesar pursued Pompey from Thessaly to Egypt, where Pompey was murdered by an officer of King Ptolemy. Caesar wintered in Alexandria, fighting with the populace and dallying with Queen Cleopatra. In 47 he fought a brief local war in northeastern Anatolia with Pharnaces, king of the Cimmerian Bosporus, who was trying to regain his father Mithradates' kingdom of Pontus. Caesar's famous words, *Veni, vidi, vici* ("I came, I saw, I conquered"), are his own account of this campaign.

Caesar then returned to Rome, but a few months later, now with the title of dictator, he left for Africa, where his opponents had rallied. In 46 he crushed their army at Thapsus and returned to Rome, only to leave in November for Farther Spain to deal with a fresh outbreak of resistance, which he crushed on March 17, 45 BCE, at Munda. He then returned to Rome to start putting the Greco-Roman world in order. He had less than a year's grace for this huge task of reconstruction before his assassination in 44 in the Senate House at Rome on March 15 (the Ides of March).

Caesar's death was partly due to his clemency and impatience, which, in combination, were dangerous for his personal security. Caesar had not hesitated to commit atrocities against "barbarians" when it had suited him, but he was almost consistently magnanimous in his treatment of his defeated Roman opponents. Thus clemency was probably not just a matter of policy. Caesar's earliest experience in his political career had been Sulla's implacable persecution of his defeated domestic opponents. Caesar amnestied his opponents wholesale and gave a number of them responsible positions in his new regime. Gaius Cassius Longinus, who was the moving spirit in the plot to murder him, and Marcus Junius Brutus, the symbolic embodiment of Roman republicanism, were both former enemies. "Et tu, Brute" ("You too, Brutus") was Caesar's expression of his particular anguish at being stabbed by a man whom he had forgiven, trusted, and loved.

There were, however, also a number of ex-Caesareans among the 60 conspirators. They had been goaded into this volte-face by the increasingly monarchical trend of Caesar's regime and, perhaps at least as much, by the aristocratic disdain that inhibited Caesar from taking any trouble to sugar the bitter pill. Some stood to lose, rather than to gain, personally by the removal of the autocrat who had made their political fortunes. But even if they were acting on principle, they were blind to the truth that the reign of the Roman nobility was broken beyond recall and that even Caesar might not have been able to overthrow the ancien régime if its destruction had not been long overdue. They also failed to recognize that by making Caesar a martyr they were creating his posthumous political fortune.

If Caesar had not been murdered in 44, he might have lived on for 15 or 20 years. His physical constitution was unusually tough, though in his last years he had several epileptic seizures. What would he have done with this time? The answer can only be guessed from what he did do in the few months available. He found time in the year 46 BCE to reform the Roman calendar. In 45 he enacted a law laying down a standard pattern for the constitutions of the municipia, which were by this time the units of local self-government in most of the territory inhabited by Roman citizens. In 59 Caesar had already resurrected the city of Capua, which the republican Roman regime more than 150 years earlier had deprived of its juridical corporate personality; he now resurrected the other two great cities, Carthage and Corinth, that his predecessors had destroyed. This was only a part of what he did to resettle his discharged soldiers and the urban proletariat of Rome. He was also generous in granting Roman citizenship to aliens. (He had given it to all of Cisalpine Gaul, north of the Po, in 49.) He increased the size of the Senate and made its personnel more representative of the whole Roman citizenry.

At his death, Caesar was on the point of starting out on a new military campaign to avenge and retrieve Crassus' disastrous defeat in 53 BCE by the Parthians. Would Caesar have succeeded in recapturing for the Greco-Roman world the extinct Seleucid monarchy's lost dominions east of the Euphrates, particularly Babylonia? The fate of Crassus' army had shown that the terrain in northern Mesopotamia favoured Parthian cavalry against Roman infantry. Would Caesar's military genius have outweighed this handicap? And would Rome's hitherto inexhaustible reservoir of military manpower have sufficed for this additional call upon it? Only guesses are possible, for Caesar's assassination condemned the Romans to another 13 years of civil war, and Rome would never again possess sufficient manpower to conquer and hold Babylonia.

PERSONALITY AND REPUTATION

Caesar was not and is not lovable. His generosity to defeated opponents, magnanimous though it was, did not

Bust of Julius Caesar. © Photos.com/Thinkstock

win their affection. He won his soldiers' devotion by the victories that his intellectual ability, applied to warfare, brought them. Yet, though not lovable, Caesar was and is attractive, indeed fascinating. His political achievement required ability, in effect amounting to genius, in several different fields, including administration and generalship besides the minor arts of wire pulling and propaganda.

In all these, Caesar was a supreme virtuoso. But if he had not also been something more than this he would not have been the supremely great man that he undoubtedly was.

Caesar was great beyond—and even in conflict with—the requirements of his political ambition. He showed a human spiritual greatness in his generosity to defeated opponents, which was partly responsible for his assassination. (The merciless Sulla abdicated and died in his bed.)

Another field in which Caesar's genius went far beyond the requirements of his political ambition was his writings. Of these, his speeches, letters, and pamphlets are lost. Only his accounts (both incomplete and supplemented by other hands) of the Gallic War and the civil war survive. Caesar ranked as a masterly public speaker in an age in which he was in competition first with Hortensius and then with Cicero.

All Caesar's speeches and writings, lost and extant, apparently served political purposes. He turned his funeral orations for his wife and for his aunt to account, for political propaganda. His accounts of his wars are subtly contrived to make the unsuspecting reader see Caesar's acts in the light that Caesar chooses. The accounts are written in the form of terse, dry, factual reports that look impersonal and objective, yet every recorded fact has been carefully selected and presented. As for the lost *Anticato*, a reply to Cicero's eulogy of Caesar's dead opponent Marcus Porcius Cato, it is a testimony to Caesar's political insight that he made the time to write it, in spite of the overwhelming military, administrative, and legislative demands on him. He realized that Cato, in giving his life for his cause (46 BCE), had made himself posthumously into a much more potent political force than he had ever been in his lifetime. Caesar was right, from his point of view, to try to put salt on Cato's tail. He did not succeed, however. For the next 150 years, Cato the martyr continued to be a nuisance, sometimes a menace, to Caesar's successors.

The mark of Caesar's genius in his writings is that though they were written for propaganda they are nevertheless of outstanding literary merit. A reader who has seen through their prosaic purpose can ignore it and appreciate them as splendid works of art.

Caesar's most amazing characteristic is his energy, intellectual and physical. He prepared his seven books on the Gallic War for publication in 51 BCE when he still had serious revolts in Gaul on his hands, and he wrote his books on the civil war and his *Anticato* in the hectic years between 49 and 44 BCE. His physical energy was of the same order. For instance, in the winter of 57–56 he found time to visit his third province, Illyria, as well as Cisalpine Gaul; and in the interval between his campaigns of 55 and 54 he transacted public business in Cisalpine Gaul and went to Illyria to settle accounts with the Pirustae, a turbulent tribe in what is now Albania. In 49 BCE he marched, within a single campaigning season, from the Rubicon to Brundisium and from Brundisium to Spain. At Alexandria, probably aged 53, he saved himself from sudden death by his prowess as a swimmer.

Caesar's physical vitality perhaps partly accounts for his sexual promiscuity, which was out of the ordinary, even by contemporary Greek and Roman standards. It was rumoured that during his first visit to the East he had had homosexual relations with King Nicomedes of Bithynia. The rumour is credible, though not proved, and was repeated throughout Caesar's life. There is no doubt of Caesar's heterosexual affairs, many of them with married women. Probably Caesar looked upon these as trivial recreations. Yet he involved himself at least twice in escapades that might have wrecked his career. If he did in fact have an affair with Pompey's wife, Mucia, he was risking his entente with Pompey. A more notorious, though not quite so hazardous, affair was his liaison with Cleopatra. By dallying with her at Alexandria, he risked losing what he had just won at Pharsalus. By allowing her to visit him in Rome in 46 BCE, he flouted public feeling and added to the list of tactless acts that, cumulatively, goaded old comrades and amnestied enemies into assassinating him.

This cool-headed man of genius with an erratic vein of sexual exuberance undoubtedly changed the course of history at the western end of the Old World. By liquidating the scandalous and bankrupt rule of the Roman nobility, he gave the Roman state—and with it the Greco-Roman civilization—a reprieve that lasted for more than 600 years in the East and for more than 400 years in the relatively backward West. Caesar substituted for the Roman oligarchy an autocracy that could never afterward be abolished. If he had not done this when he did it, Rome and the Greco-Roman world might have succumbed, before the beginning of the Christian era, to barbarian invaders in the West and to the Parthian Empire in the East. The prolongation of the life of the Greco-Roman civilization had important historical effects. Under the Roman Empire the Near East was impregnated with Hellenism for six or seven more centuries. But for this the Hellenic element might not have been present in sufficient strength to make its decisive impact on Christianity and Islam. Gaul, too, would have sunk deeper into barbarism when the Franks overran it, if it had not been associated with the civilized Mediterranean world for more than 500 years as a result of Caesar's conquest.

Caesar's political achievement was limited. Its effects were confined to the western end of the Old World and were comparatively short-lived by Chinese or ancient Egyptian standards. The Chinese state founded by Shihuangdi in the 3rd century BCE still stands, and its future may be still greater than its past. Yet, even if Caesar were to prove to have been of lesser stature than this Chinese colossus, he would still remain a giant by comparison with the common run of human beings.

FAXIAN

(fl. 399–414 CE)

Faxian (or Fa-hsien) was a Chinese Buddhist monk, whose pilgrimage to India in 402 initiated Sino-Indian relations and whose writings give important information about early Buddhism. After his return to China he translated into Chinese the many Sanskrit Buddhist texts he had brought back.

Sehi—his original name; he later adopted the spiritual name Faxian ("Splendour of Dharma")—was born at Shanxi during the 4th century CE. Living at the time of the Dong (Eastern) Jin dynasty, when Buddhism enjoyed an imperial favour seldom equalled in Chinese history, he was stirred by a profound faith to go to India, the "Holy Land" of Buddhism, in order to visit the sites of the Buddha's life and to bring back Buddhist texts that were still unknown in China.

The historical importance of Faxian is twofold. On the one hand, a famous record of his journeys— *Foguoji* ("Record of Buddhist Kingdoms")—contains valuable information not found elsewhere concerning the history of Indian Buddhism during the early centuries CE. Because of the fairly detailed descriptions by Faxian, it is possible to envision Buddhist India before the Muslim invasions. On the other hand, he strengthened Chinese Buddhism by helping provide a better knowledge of Buddhist sacred texts. After studying them for 10 years in India, he brought back to China a great number of copies of Buddhist texts and translated them from Sanskrit into Chinese. Among them, two of the most important were the *Mahaparinirvana-sutra*, a text glorifying the eternal, personal, and pure nature of nirvana—on which the nirvana school in China then based its doctrines—and the Vinaya (rules of discipline for the monks) of the Mahasanghika school, which thus became available for the regulation of the numerous monastic communities in China.

Faxian first crossed the trackless wastes of Central Asia. His trip across the desert he recalled in a terrifying way:

> *In the desert were numerous evil spirits and scorching winds, causing death to anyone who would meet them. Above there were no birds, while on the ground there were no animals. One looked as far as one could in all directions for a path to cross, but there was none to choose. Only the dried bones of the dead served as indications.*

After arriving at Khotan, an oasis centre for caravans, he defied the terrors of snow during his crossing of the Pamirs; the mountain path was terribly narrow and steep:

The path was difficult and rocky and ran along a cliff extremely steep. The mountain itself was just one sheer wall of rock 8,000 feet (2,438 metres) high, and as one approached it, one became dizzy. If one wished to advance, there was no place for him to place his feet. Below was the Indus River. In former times people had chiseled a path out of the rocks and distributed on the face of the cliff over 700 ladders for the descent.

(Kenneth K.S. Ch'en, *Buddhism in China: A Historical Survey*, Princeton University Press, 1964)

In northwestern India, which he entered in 402, Faxian visited the most important seats of Buddhist learning: Udyana, Gandhara, Peshawar, and Taxila. Above all, however, he was attracted by eastern India, where the Buddha had spent his life and had taught his doctrines. His pilgrimage was completed by visits to the most holy spots: Kapilavastu, where the Buddha was born; Bodh Gaya, where the Buddha acquired the supreme enlightenment; Banaras (Varanasi), where the Buddha preached his first sermon; and Kushinagara, where the Buddha entered into the perfect nirvana.

Faxian then stayed for a long time at Pataliputra, conversing with Buddhist monks, studying Sanskrit texts with Buddhist scholars, and transcribing the Vinaya of the Mahasanghika school—a dissident group of the Hinayana (Lesser Vehicle) born from the Council of Vesali (*c.* 383 BCE). He also acquired another version of the Vinaya worked out by the Sarvastivada school—an early Buddhist group that taught the equal reality of all mental states (past, present, and future)—and the famous *Mahaparinirvana-sutra*. When he had deepened his knowledge of Buddhism and was in possession of sacred texts that were not yet translated into Chinese, he decided to go back to China. Instead of once more taking the overland route, however,

Faxian took the sea route, first sailing to Ceylon (now Sri Lanka), at that time one of the most flourishing centres of Buddhist studies. There, by securing the Mahishasaka Vinaya—a recension of the Hinayana Vinaya—and a selection of the Sarvastivada canon, he added to the number of Buddhist texts that he had collected.

After a two-year stay in Ceylon, he set sail for China, but the perils of the sea were as great as the hardships and dangers of desert and mountain he had faced in coming to India. A violent storm drove his ship onto an island that was probably Java. He took another boat bound for Canton (now Guangzhou). Instead of landing at the south China port, Faxian's ship was driven astray by another storm and was finally blown to a port on the Shandong Peninsula. In all, Faxian spent more than 200 days at sea. After returning to his homeland, Faxian resumed his scholarly tasks and translated into Chinese the Buddhist texts he had taken so much trouble to bring back.

SAINT BRENDAN

(b. c. 484/486, Tralee [now in County Kerry], Ireland—d. 578, Annaghdown, County Galway; feast day May 16)

The 6th-century-CE Celtic saint Brendan (Brandon or Branden; Gaelic Brénaind) was a monastic founder, abbot, and hero of legendary voyages in the Atlantic Ocean. Reputedly raised and educated by Abbess St. Ita at her boys' school in what later became County Limerick, he later studied under Abbot St. Jarlath of Tuam. After becoming a monk and priest, he was entrusted with the abbey of Ardfert and subsequently established monasteries in Ireland and Scotland, the chief one being Clúain Ferta Brénaind (Anglicized Clonfert), founded in 561.

Statue of Saint Brendan, Bantry, Ireland. El Gringo

He is often called Brendan of Clonfert to distinguish him from several namesakes, and he also is known by the names Brendan the Voyager and Brendan the Navigator.

A noted traveler, Brendan voyaged to the Hebrides (according to St. Adamnan's life of Abbot St. Columba of Iona) and to western Scotland and perhaps to Wales and Brittany. Later, possibly as early as the 8th century, Brendan was immortalized as the hero of a legendary Christian tale of sea adventure, *Navigatio Brendani* ("Voyage of Brendan"). This Irish epic, a narrative masterpiece, was translated into Latin prose early in the 10th century. According to the *Navigatio*, Brendan makes an astonishing Atlantic journey with other monks to the "Promised Land of the Saints" (later identified possibly as the Canary Islands), which he reaches after a prolonged search. St. Brendan's Island, somewhere in the Atlantic and long sought by sailors, was believed in Columbus's time to have been sighted by inhabitants of the Azores, probably the effect of mirage.

XUANZANG

(b. 602, Goushi, Luozhou [now Yanshi, Henan province], China—d. 664, Chang'an [now Xi'an], China)

Xuanzang (or Hsüan-tsang) was a Buddhist monk and Chinese pilgrim to India who translated the sacred scriptures of Buddhism from Sanskrit into Chinese and founded in China the Buddhist Consciousness Only school. His fame rests mainly on the volume and diversity of his translations of the Buddhist sutras and on the record of his travels in Central Asia and India, which, with its wealth of detailed and precise data, has been of inestimable value to historians and archaeologists. His original name was Chen Yi, and he was also known by the names Muchatipo (Sanskrit Mokshadeva) and Yuanzhang and by the honorary epithet Sanzang.

He was born into a family in which there had been scholars for generations and received a classical Confucian education in his youth. Under the influence of an older brother, however, he became interested in the Buddhist scriptures and was soon converted to Buddhism. With his brother he traveled to Chang'an and then to Sichuan to escape the political turmoil that gripped China at that time. While in Sichuan, Xuanzang began studying Buddhist philosophy but was soon troubled by numerous discrepancies and contradictions in the texts. Not finding any solution from his Chinese masters, he decided to go to India to study at the fountainhead of Buddhism.

Unable to obtain a travel permit, he left Chang'an by stealth in 629. On his journey he traveled north of the Takla Makan Desert, passing through such oasis centres as Turfan, Karashar, Kucha, Tashkent, and Samarkand, then beyond the Iron Gates into Bactria, across the Hindu Kush (mountains) into Kapisha, Gandhara, and Kashmir in northwestern India. From there he sailed down the Ganges River to Mathura, then on to the holy land of Buddhism in the eastern reaches of the Ganges, where he arrived in 633.

In India, Xuanzang visited all the sacred sites connected with the life of the Buddha, and he journeyed along the east and west coasts of the subcontinent. The major portion of his time, however, was spent at the Nalanda monastery, the great Buddhist centre of learning, where he

Bronze statue of the Chinese explorer and Buddhist monk Xuanzang, outside a temple in Shaanxi province, China. Cupertino/Shutterstock.com

perfected his knowledge of Sanskrit, Buddhist philosophy, and Indian thought. While he was in India, Xuanzang's reputation as a scholar became so great that even the powerful king Harsha, ruler of northern India, wanted to meet and honour him. Thanks largely to that king's patronage, Xuanzang's return trip to China, begun in 643, was greatly facilitated.

Xuanzang returned to Chang'an (by then the capital of the Tang dynasty) in 645, after an absence of 16 years. He was accorded a tumultuous welcome at the capital, and a few days later he was received in audience by the emperor, who was so enthralled by his accounts of foreign lands that he offered the Buddhist monk a ministerial post. Xuanzang, however, preferred to serve his religion, so he respectfully declined the imperial offer.

Xuanzang spent the remainder of his life translating the Buddhist scriptures, numbering 657 items packed in 520 cases, that he brought back from India. He was able to translate only a small portion of this huge volume, about 75 items in 1,335 chapters, but his translations included some of the most important Mahayana scriptures.

Xuanzang's main interest centred on the philosophy of the Yogacara (Vijnanavada) school, and he and his disciple Kuiji (632–682) were responsible for the formation of the Weishi (Consciousness Only school) in China. Its doctrine was set forth in Xuanzang's *Chengweishilun* ("Treatise on the Establishment of the Doctrine of Consciousness Only"), a translation of the essential Yogacara writings, and in Kuijhi's commentary. The main thesis of this school is that the whole world is but a representation of the mind. While Xuanzang and Kuiji lived, the school achieved some degree of eminence and popularity, but with the passing of the two masters the school rapidly declined. Before that happened, however, a Japanese monk named Dōshō arrived in China in 653 to study under Xuanzang, and, after he had completed his study, he returned to Japan to introduce the doctrines of the Ideation Only school in that country. During the 7th and 8th centuries, that school, called Hossō by the Japanese, became the most influential of all the Buddhist schools in Japan.

In addition to his translations, Xuanzang composed the *Datang-Xiyu-Ji* ("Records of the Western Regions of the Great Tang Dynasty"), the great record of the various countries passed through during his journey. Out of veneration for this intrepid and devout Buddhist monk and pilgrim, the Tang emperor canceled all audiences for three days after Xuanzang's death.

ELDAD THE DANITE

(fl. 9th century)

The Jewish traveler and philologist Eldad the Danite (Hebrew Eldad ben Mahli ha-Dani) was generally credited with the authorship of a fanciful geographical narrative that exerted an enduring influence throughout the Middle Ages. This possibly gave rise to the legend of Prester John, the mighty Asian priest-potentate of fabulous wealth and power.

Probably originally from southern Arabia, Eldad visited Mesopotamia, Egypt, North Africa, and Spain and caused a stir by his account of the Ten Lost Tribes of Israel. He himself claimed to be a descendant of the Danites, who, together with the tribes of Naphtali, Asher, and Gad, were said to have established a Jewish kingdom in Cush (Kush), variously interpreted as Ethiopia or, roughly, present-day Sudan. His veracity was challenged largely because the ritual prescriptions he described diverged from those of the Talmud, the rabbinical compendium of law, lore, and commentary. His Hebrew narrative, *Sefer Eldad*, established his reputation as a philologist whom leading medieval Jewish grammarians and lexicographers quoted as an authority on linguistic difficulties. It appeared in several languages and in widely deviating versions. The first edition was published at the Italian city of Mantua in 1480.

AL-MASʿŪDĪ

(b. 9th century, Baghdad, Iraq—d. 957, Al-Fusṭāṭ, Egypt)

Abū al-Ḥusayn ʿAlī ibn al-Ḥusayn al-Masʿūdī was a historian and traveler who became known as the "Herodotus of the Arabs." He was the first Arab to combine history and scientific geography in a large-scale work, *Murūj al-dhahab wa maʿādin al-jawāhir* ("The Meadows of Gold and Mines of Gems"), a world history.

As a child, al-Masʿūdī showed an extraordinary love of learning, an excellent memory, a capacity to write quickly, and a boundless curiosity that led him to study a wide variety of subjects, ranging from history and geography—his main interests—to comparative religion and science. He was not content to learn merely from books and teachers but traveled widely to gain firsthand knowledge of the countries about which he wrote. His travels extended to

Syria, Iran, Armenia, the shores of the Caspian Sea, the Indus Valley, Ceylon (now Sri Lanka), Oman in Arabia, and the east coast of Africa as far south as Zanzibar, at least, and, possibly, Madagascar.

The titles of more than 20 books attributed to him are known, including several about Islamic beliefs and sects and even one about poisons, but most of his writings have been lost. His major work was *Akhbār al-zamān* ("The History of Time") in 30 volumes. This seems to have been an encyclopaedic world history, taking in not only political history but also many facets of human knowledge and activity. A manuscript of one volume of this work is said to be preserved in Vienna; if this manuscript is genuine, it is all that has remained of the work. Al-Masʿūdī followed it with *Kitāb al-awsaṭ* ("Book of the Middle"), variously described as a supplement to or an abridgment of the *Akhbār al-zamān*. The *Kitāb* is undoubtedly a chronological history. A manuscript in the Bodleian Library, Oxford, may possibly be one volume of it.

Neither of these works had much effect on scholars — in the case of *Akhbār al-zamān*, possibly because of its daunting length. So al-Masʿūdī rewrote the two combined works in less detail in a single book, to which he gave the fanciful title of *Murūj al-dhahab wa maʿ ā din al-jawāhir* ("The Meadows of Gold and the Mines of Gems"). This book quickly became famous and established the author's reputation as a leading historian. Ibn Khaldūn, the great 14th-century Arab philosopher of history, describes al-Masʿūdī as an imam ("leader," or "example") for historians. Though an abridgment, *Murūj al-dhahab* is still a substantial work. In his introduction, al-Masʿūdī lists more than 80 historical works known to him, but he also stresses the importance of his travels to "learn the peculiarities of various nations and parts of the world." He claims that, in the book, he has dealt with every subject that may be useful or interesting.

The work is in 132 chapters. The second half is a straightforward history of Islam, beginning with the Prophet Muhammad, then dealing with the caliphs down to al-Mas'ūdī's own time, one by one. While it often makes interesting reading because of its vivid description and entertaining anecdotes, this part of the book is superficial. It is seldom read now, as much better accounts can be found elsewhere, particularly in the writings of al-Ṭabarī.

The first half, in contrast, is of great value, though somewhat sprawling and confused in its design. It starts with the creation of the world and Jewish history. Then it intersperses chapters describing the history, geography, social life, and religious customs of non-Islamic lands, such as India, Greece, and Rome, with accounts of the oceans, the calendars of various nations, climate, the solar system, and great temples. Among particularly interesting sections are those on pearl diving in the Persian Gulf, amber found in East Africa, Hindu burial customs, the land route to China, and navigation, with its various hazards, such as storms and waterspouts. The relative positions and characteristics of the seas are also explained.

Al-Mas'ūdī's approach to his task was original: he gave as much weight to social, economic, religious, and cultural matters as to politics. Moreover, he utilized information obtained from sources not previously regarded as reliable. He retailed what he learned from merchants, local writers (including non-Muslims), and others he met on his travels. He displayed interest in all religions, including Hinduism and Zoroastrianism, as well as Judaism and Christianity. However, he tended to reproduce uncritically what he heard; thus, his explanations of natural phenomena are often incorrect. Yet he was no worse, in this respect, than medieval European travelers such as Marco Polo and Sir John Mandeville.

Al-Masʿūdī had no settled abode for most of his adult life. In 945 he settled in Damascus. Two years later, he left there for al-Fusṭāṭ (old Cairo), where he remained until his death in 957. It was there, in the last year of his life, that he wrote *Kitāb al-tanbīh wa al-ishrāf* ("The Book of Notification and Verification"), in which he summarized, corrected, and brought up-to-date the contents of his former writings, especially the three historical works.

AL-HAMDĀNĪ

(b. 893? Sanaa, Yemen—d. c. 945?)

The chief fame of the Arab geographer, poet, grammarian, historian, and astronomer Abū Muḥammad al-Ḥasan ibn Aḥmad al-Hamdānī derives from his authoritative writings on South Arabian history and geography. From his literary production he was known as the "tongue of South Arabia." Most of al-Hamdānī's life was spent in Arabia itself. He was widely educated, and he traveled extensively, acquiring a broad knowledge of his country. He became involved in a number of political controversies. When he was imprisoned for one of them, his influence was sufficient to invoke a tribal rebellion on his behalf to secure his release.

His encyclopaedia *Al-Iklīl* ("The Crown"; Eng. trans. of vol. 8 by N.A. Faris as *The Antiquities of South Arabia*) and his other writings are a major source of information on Arabia, providing a valuable anthology of South Arabian poetry as well as much genealogical, topographical, and historical information. *Al-Dāmighah* ("The Cleaving"), a *qaṣīdah*, is perhaps his most famous poem; in it he defends his own southern tribe, the Hamdān. It has been said that al-Hamdānī died in prison in Sanaa in 945, but this is now in question.

ERIK THE RED

(fl. 10th century, Norway)

The Norseman Erik the Red (Norwegian Eirik Raude) was the founder of the first European settlement on Greenland (*c.* 986). He was also the father of Leif Eriksson, one of the first Europeans to reach North America.

As a child, Erik left his native Norway for western Iceland with his father, Thorvald, who had been exiled for manslaughter. In the Scandinavian style of the time he was known as Erik Thorvaldson (Norwegian Eirik Torvaldsson) and in his youth was nicknamed Erik the Red. When Erik was similarly exiled from Iceland about 980, he decided to explore the land to the west (Greenland). That land, visible in distorted form because of the effect of looming (a type of mirage) from the mountaintops of western Iceland, lay across 175 miles (280 km) of water; it had been skirted by the Norwegian Gunnbjörn Ulfsson earlier in the 10th century. Erik sailed in 982 with his household and livestock but was unable to approach the coast because of drift ice. The party rounded the southern tip of Greenland and settled in an area near present Julianehåb (Qaqortoq). During the three-year period of Erik's exile, the settlers

Engraving depicting the arrival of the Norse explorer Erik the Red and his crew at the territory that became known as Greenland. Mansell/Time & Life Pictures/Getty Images

encountered no other people, though they explored to the northwest, discovering Disko Island (now Qeqertarsuaq).

Erik returned to Iceland in 986. His descriptions of the territory, which he named Greenland, convinced many people anxious for more habitable land to join a return expedition. Of the 25 ships that sailed from Iceland, only 14 ships and 350 colonists are believed to have landed safely at an area later known as Eystribygdh (Eastern Colony). By the year 1000 there were an estimated 1,000 Scandinavian settlers in the colony, but an epidemic in 1002 considerably reduced the population. Erik's colony, commemorated in the Icelandic *Eiríks saga* ("Saga of Erik"), gradually died out; but other Norse settlements in Greenland continued and maintained contact with Norway until the 15th century, when communications stopped for more than 100 years.

LEIF ERIKSSON THE LUCKY

fl. 11th century)

The Norse explorer Leif Eriksson, or Ericson (Norwegian Leiv Eriksson den Hepne, Icelandic Leifur Eiríksson), is widely held to have been among the first Europeans to reach the shores of North America. The 13th- and 14th-century Icelandic accounts of his life and additional later evidence show that he was certainly a member of an early Viking voyage to North America, but it remains doubtful whether he led the initial expedition.

The second of three sons of Erik the Red, the first European colonizer of Greenland, Leif sailed from Greenland to Norway in 1000, according to the Icelandic *Eiríks saga* ("Saga of Erik"), and was there converted to Christianity by the Norwegian king Olaf I Tryggvason. The following year Leif was commissioned by Olaf to urge Christianity upon the Greenland settlers. He sailed off course on the return voyage and landed on the North American continent, at a region (thought to lie somewhere between Labrador and Nova Scotia) he called Vinland— perhaps because of the wild grapes and fertile land he found there. On returning to Greenland, he proselytized for Christianity and converted his mother, who built the first Christian church in Greenland, at Brattahild.

According to the *Grænlendinga saga* (*Grænlendinga saga*; "Tale of the Greenlanders") in the *Flateyjarbók* ("Songbook"), considered more reliable than the *Eiríks saga* by many modern scholars, Leif learned of Vinland

Statue depicting Leif Eriksson, looking out to sea along the shore of southern Greenland. Bernard van Dierendonck/LOOK/Getty Images

from the Icelander Bjarni Herjulfsson, who had been there 14 years earlier. The *saga* pictures Leif as reaching North America several years after 1000 and visiting Helluland (possibly Labrador) and Markland (possibly Newfoundland) as well as Vinland. Further expeditions to Vinland were then made by Thorvald, Leif's brother, and by the Icelander Thorfinn Karlsefni.

THORFINN KARLSEFNI

(b. 980, Iceland—d. after 1007)

The Icelandic-born Scandinavian Thorfinn Karlsefni was the leader of an early colonizing expedition to North America. His travels were recounted in the *Eiríks saga* ("Saga of Erik") and the *Groenlendinga saga* (*Grænlendinga saga*; "Tale of the Greenlanders").

Thorfinn must have been given his nickname, Karlsefni, at an early age, since it means "promising boy." His grandfather in about 900 had led many Norse to colonize Iceland, and by 986 their descendants felt so hard-pressed for stock-farming land there that they followed the lead of Erik the Red and migrated to Greenland. Thorfinn, who was a successful trader and sea captain, reached what was known as the eastern settlement of Greenland with a group of colonists in 1003. There he married Gudrid, who was the widow of one of Erik the Red's sons, Thorstein.

Thorfinn and Gudrid were persuaded by Erik to lead an expedition to Vinland (believed to be in the area of present-day Newfoundland and Labrador and Nova Scotia), which had been reached for the first time three years earlier by another of Erik's sons, Leif Eriksson. In about 1004 the couple set out with about 130 people in three ships and sailed westward, possibly making their first landfall on the North American continent at Baffin Island. They followed the coastline southward until they reached a heavily wooded region, perhaps some part of the Gulf of St. Lawrence shore, and settled there to engage in haymaking, hunting, and fishing. Thorfinn's and Gudrid's son, Snorri (born *c.* 1005), was the first European born on the North American mainland.

That first winter the Scandinavian colonists met no people, but the next summer they were visited by friendly native peoples who were probably Inuit (Eskimo). The next summer they were visited by more numerous and less friendly natives, and fighting ensued, which the Scandinavians won but at the cost of some lives. Three years after the landing, Thorfinn and the rest of the colonists abandoned Vinland and returned to Greenland. Later they returned to Iceland. L'Anse aux Meadows, an archaeological site at the northern tip on Newfoundland island, has been associated with the Vinland colonists.

AL-SHARĪF AL-IDRĪSĪ

(b. 1100, Sabtah, Morocco—d. 1165/66, Sicily
or Sabtah)

The Arab traveler and geographer Abū 'Abd Allāh Muḥammad ibn Muḥammad ibn 'Abd Allāh ibn Idrīs al-Ḥammūdī al-Ḥasanī al-Idrīsī—commonly known as al-Sharīf al-Idrīsī or, simply, al-Idrīsī—was an adviser to Roger II, the Norman king of Sicily. He wrote one of the greatest works of medieval geography, *Kitāb nuzhat al-mushtāq fī ikhtirāq al-āfāq* ("The Pleasure Excursion of One Who Is Eager to Traverse the Regions of the World").

Al-Idrīsī traced his descent through a long line of princes, caliphs, and holy men to the Prophet Muhammad.

Portrait of the Arab geographer al-Sharīf al-Idrīsī, whose writings and maps opened up whole new worlds during medieval times. Gianni Dagli Orti/The Art Archive at Art Resource, NY

His immediate forebears, the Ḥammūdids of the short-lived caliphate (1016–58) in Spain and North Africa, were an offshoot of the Idrīsids of Morocco (789–985), a dynasty descended from Muhammad's eldest grandson, al-Ḥasan ibn ʿAlī.

Few facts are known about al-Idrīsī's life. He was born in Sabtah (now Ceuta, a Spanish exclave on the coast of Morocco), where his Ḥammūdī ancestors had fled after the fall of Málaga, their last foothold in Spain, in 1057. He spent much of his early life traveling in North Africa and Spain and seems to have acquired detailed and accurate information on both regions. He is known to have studied in Córdoba for a number of years and also to have lived in Marrakesh, Morocco, and Qusṭanṭinah (Constantine), Algeria. Apparently his travels took him to many parts of western Europe, including Portugal, northern Spain, the French Atlantic coast, and southern England. He visited Asia Minor (Anatolia) when he was barely 16 years old.

In about 1145, while still at the peak of his powers, al-Idrīsī entered the service of Roger II of Sicily—a step that marked a turning point in his career. Henceforward, all his great achievements were to be indissolubly linked to the Norman court at Palermo, where he lived and worked for the rest of his life. Some Western scholars have suggested that al-Idrīsī may have been regarded as a renegade by other Muslims for entering the service of a Christian king and praising him lavishly in his writings. Moreover, some writers have attributed the paucity of biographical information on al-Idrīsī in Muslim sources to these circumstances.

There has always been uncertainty about al-Idrīsī's reasons for going to Sicily. It has been suggested that he may have been induced to do so by some of his Ḥammūdī kinsmen, who are known to have settled there and who, according to the Spanish-Arab traveler Ibn Jubayr

(1145–1217), enjoyed great power and prestige among Sicilian Muslims. According to the 14th-century Arab scholar al-Ṣafadī, Roger II invited al-Idrīsī to Sicily to make a map of the world for him, telling him:

> *You are a member of the caliphal family. For that reason, when you happen to be among Muslims, their kings will seek to kill you, whereas when you are with me you are assured of the safety of your person.*

Al-Idrīsī agreed to stay, and Roger provided him with a king's pension.

Al-Idrīsī's service in Sicily resulted in the completion of three major geographic works: (1) a silver planisphere on which was depicted a map of the world, (2) a world map consisting of 70 sections formed by dividing the Earth north of the Equator into 7 climatic zones of equal width, each of which was subdivided into 10 equal parts by lines of longitude, and (3) a geographic text intended as a key to the planisphere. This was his great work of descriptive geography, known as *Kitāb nuzhat al-mushtāq fī ikhtirāq al-āfāq* and also as *Kitā Rujār*, or *Al-Kitāb ar-Rujārī* ("The Book of Roger"). In compiling it, al-Idrīsī combined material from Arabic and Greek geographic works with information obtained through firsthand observation and eyewitness reports. The king and his Arab geographer chose a number of persons, including men skilled in drawing, and dispatched them to various countries to observe and record what they saw. Al-Idrīsī completed the book in January 1154, shortly before Roger's death.

The silver planisphere has been lost, but the maps and book have survived. A German scholar, Konrad Miller, published the maps in his *Mappe Arabicae* (1926–31), and later an emended world map, based upon Miller's work, was published by the Iraq Academy (Baghdad, 1951). A critical edition of al-Idrīsī's *Kitāb nuzhat al-mushtāq*, undertaken by a committee of Italian scholars in cooperation with a group of international experts, appeared in the 1970s.

Kitāb nuzhat al-mushtāq represents a serious attempt to combine descriptive and astronomical geography. That this effort was not an unqualified success apparently stems from the author's inadequate mastery of the physical and mathematical aspects of geography. He has been criticized not only for failing to make use of the important geographic contributions of other scientists of his times, such as the 11th-century Arab scholar al-Bīrūnī, but also for his uncritical use of earlier Greek and Arab sources. Nevertheless, al-Idrīsī's book is a major geographic monument. It is particularly valuable for its data on such regions as the Mediterranean basin and the Balkans.

A number of other geographic works are attributed to al-Idrīsī, including one (now lost) written for William I, Roger's son and successor who reigned from 1154 to 1166, as well as several critical revisions and abridgments. The Medici press in Rome published an abridgment of *Kitāb nuzhat al-mushtāq* in 1592; a Latin translation was published under the title *Geographia Nubiensis*. A complete translation of the work in French is P.A. Jaubert's two-volume *Géographie d'Édrisi* (1836–40); it is unreliable, however, because it was based on faulty manuscripts. Al-Idrīsī's scientific interests embraced medical matters as well, and his *Kitāb al-adwiya al-mufradah* ("Book of Simple Drugs"), in which he lists the names of drugs in as many as 12 languages, demonstrates the range of his linguistic abilities. Al-Idrīsī seems to have had a good knowledge of Arabic literature, and—judging by some of his verse that has survived—he was also an accomplished poet. No details are known about the last years of his life.

BENJAMIN OF TUDELA

(b. 12th century, Navarre [France])

The rabbi Benjamin of Tudela was the first known European traveler to approach the frontiers of China. His account of his journey, *Massaʻot* (*The Itinerary of Benjamin of Tudela*, 1907), illuminates the situation of Jews in Europe and Asia in the 12th century.

Motivated by commercial interests as well as a desire to learn of the conditions of Jews, he spent about 13 years journeying through Italy, Greece, Palestine, Persia, and the western borders of China, returning by way of Egypt and Sicily (1159–73). Though the *Itinerary* contains errors and treats places he may not have visited, it remains valuable.

Rabbi and traveler Benjamin of Tudela, depicted on camelback during a journey across the Sahara Desert. © Pantheon/SuperStock

MADOG AB OWAIN GWYNEDD

(fl. 1170)

The legendary voyager to America Madog (or Madoc) Ab Owain Gwynedd was a son (if he existed at all) of Owain Gwynedd (died 1170), prince of Gwynedd, in North Wales. A quarrel among Owain's sons over the distribution of their late father's estate led Madog to sail to Ireland and then westward. In a year or so he returned to Wales and assembled a group to colonize the land he had discovered. The party sailed west in 10 ships and was not seen again.

The oldest extant accounts of Madog are in Richard Hakluyt's *Voyages* (1582) and David Powel's *The Historie of Cambria* (1584). Hakluyt believed Madog had landed in Florida. In *Letters and Notes on the Manners, Customs, and Condition of the North American Indians* (1841), George Catlin surmised that Madog's expedition had reached the upper Missouri River valley and that its members were the ancestors of the Mandan Indians. There is a tradition of a "white Indian" settlement at Louisville, Kentucky, and several 17th- and 18th-century reports were published concerning encounters of frontiersmen with Welsh-speaking Indians. Most anthropologists reject the idea of pre-Columbian European contacts with American Indians, but the evidence is not conclusive. The story is the basis of the epic poem *Madoc* (1805) by the English poet Robert Southey.

GENGHIS KHAN

(b. 1162, near Lake Baikal, Mongolia—d. August 18, 1227)

The Mongolian warrior-ruler Genghis Khan, one of the most famous conquerors of history, consolidated tribes into a unified Mongolia and then extended his empire across Asia to the Adriatic Sea. Given his achievements and those of his successors, he is in the company of other great warrior-adventurers throughout history such as Alexander the Great and Julius Caesar. The name Genghis is spelled several ways, including Chinggis, Chingis, Jenghiz, and Jinghis.

Statue of the Mongolian warrior, leader, and explorer Genghis Khan. Qian/Shutterstock.com

Genghis Khan was a warrior and ruler of genius who, starting from obscure and insignificant beginnings, brought all the nomadic tribes of Mongolia under the rule of himself and his family in a rigidly disciplined military state. He then turned his attention toward the settled peoples beyond the

A 16th-century illustration showing Genghis Khan (top, centre) praying to the sun before battle, from the book The History of the Mogols. Werner Forman/Hulton Fine Art Collection/Getty Images

borders of his nomadic realm and began the series of campaigns of plunder and conquest that eventually carried the Mongol armies as far as the Adriatic Sea in one direction and the Pacific coast of China in the other, leading to the establishment of the great Mongol Empire.

HISTORICAL BACKGROUND

With the exception of the sagalike *Secret History of the Mongols* (mid-13th century), only non-Mongol sources provide near-contemporary information about the life of Genghis Khan. Almost all writers, even those who were in the Mongol service, have dwelt on the enormous destruction wrought by the Mongol invasions. One Arab historian openly expressed his horror at the recollection of them. Beyond the reach of the Mongols and relying on second-hand information, the 13th-century chronicler Matthew Paris called them a "detestable nation of Satan that poured out like devils from Tartarus so that they are rightly called Tartars." He was making a play on words with the classical word Tartarus (Hell) and the ancient tribal name of Tatar borne by some of the nomads, but his account catches the terror that the Mongols evoked. As the founder of the Mongol nation, the organizer of the Mongol armies, and the genius behind their campaigns, Genghis Khan must share the reputation of his people, even though his generals were frequently operating on their own, far from direct supervision. Nevertheless, it would be mistaken to see the Mongol campaigns as haphazard incursions by bands of marauding savages. Nor is it true, as some have supposed, that these campaigns were somehow brought about by a progressive desiccation of Inner Asia that compelled the nomads to look for new pastures. Nor, again, were the Mongol invasions a unique event. Genghis Khan was neither the first nor the last nomadic conqueror to burst out of the steppe and terrorize the settled periphery of Eurasia. His campaigns were merely larger in scale, more successful, and more lasting in effect than those of other leaders. They impinged more violently upon those sedentary peoples who had the habit of recording events in writing, and they affected a greater part of the Eurasian continent and a variety of different societies.

Two societies were in constant contact, two societies that were mutually hostile, if only because of their diametrically opposed ways of life, and yet these societies were interdependent. The nomads needed some of the staple products of the south and coveted its luxuries. These could be had by trade, by taxing transient caravans, or by armed raids. The settled peoples of China needed the products of the steppe to a lesser extent, but they could not ignore the presence of the nomadic barbarians and were forever preoccupied with resisting encroachment by one means or another. A strong dynasty, such as the 17th-century Manchu, could extend its military power directly over all Inner Asia. At other times the Chinese would have to play off one set of barbarians against another, transferring their support and juggling their alliances so as to prevent any one tribe from becoming too strong.

The cycle of dynastic strength and weakness in China was accompanied by another cycle, that of unity and fragmentation among the peoples of the steppe. At the peak of their power, a nomadic tribe under a determined leader could subjugate the other tribes to its will and, if the situation in China was one of weakness, might extend its power well beyond the steppe. In the end this extension of nomadic power over the incompatible, sedentary culture of the south brought its own nemesis. The nomads lost their traditional basis of superiority—that lightning mobility that required little in the way of supply and fodder—and were swallowed up by the Chinese they had conquered. The cycle would then be resumed; a powerful China would reemerge, and disarray and petty squabbling among ephemeral chieftains would be the new pattern of life among the nomads. The history of the Mongol conquests illustrates this analysis perfectly, and it is against this background of political contrasts and tensions that the life of Genghis Khan must be evaluated. His campaigns were not an inexplicable natural or even God-given catastrophe but the outcome of a set of circumstances manipulated by a soldier of ambition, determination, and genius. He found his tribal world ready for unification, at a time when China and other settled states were, for one reason or another, simultaneously in decline, and he exploited the situation.

EARLY STRUGGLES

Various dates are given for the birth of Temüjin (or Temuchin), as Genghis Khan was named—after a leader who was defeated by his father, Yesügei, when Temüjin was born. The chronology of Temüjin's early life is uncertain. He may have been born in 1155, in 1162 (the date favoured today in Mongolia), or in 1167. According to legend, his birth was auspicious, because he came into the world holding a clot of blood in his hand. He is also said to have been of divine origin, his first ancestor having been a gray wolf, "born with a destiny from heaven on high." Yet his early years were anything but promising. When he was nine, Yesügei, a member of the royal Borjigin clan of the Mongols, was poisoned by a band of Tatars, another nomadic people, in continuance of an old feud.

With Yesügei dead, the remainder of the clan, led by the rival Taychiut family, abandoned his widow, Höelün, and her children, considering them too weak to exercise leadership and seizing the opportunity to usurp power. For a time the small family led a life of extreme poverty, eating roots and fish instead of the normal nomad diet of mutton and mare's milk. Two anecdotes illustrate both Temüjin's straitened circumstances and, more significantly, the power he already had of attracting supporters through sheer force of personality. Once he was captured by the Taychiut, who, rather than killing him, kept him around their camps, wearing a wooden collar. One night, when they were feasting, Temüjin, noticing that he was being ineptly guarded, knocked down the sentry with a blow from his wooden collar and fled. The Taychiut searched all night for him, and he was seen by one of their people, who, impressed by the fire in his eyes, did not denounce him but helped him escape at the risk of his own life. On another occasion horse thieves came and stole eight of the nine horses that the small family owned. Temüjin pursued them. On the way he stopped to ask a young stranger, called Bo'orchu, if he had seen the horses. Bo'orchu immediately left the milking he was engaged in, gave Temüjin a fresh horse, and set out with him to help recover the lost beasts. He refused any reward but, recognizing Temüjin's authority, attached himself irrevocably to him as a *nökör*, or free companion, abandoning his own family.

Temüjin and his family apparently preserved a considerable fund of prestige as members of the royal Borjigin clan, in spite of their rejection by it. Among other things, he was able to claim the wife to whom Yesügei had betrothed him just before his death. But the Merkit people, a tribe living in northern Mongolia, bore Temüjin a grudge, because Yesügei had stolen his own wife, Höelün, from one of their men, and in their turn they ravished Temüjin's wife Börte. Temüjin felt able to appeal to Toghril, khan of the Kereit tribe, with whom Yesügei had had the relationship of *anda*, or sworn brother, and at that time the most powerful Mongol prince, for help in recovering Börte. He had had the foresight to rekindle this friendship by presenting Toghril with a sable skin, which he himself had received as a bridal gift. He seems to have had nothing else to offer; yet, in exchange; Toghril promised to reunite Temüjin's scattered people, and he is said to have redeemed his promise by furnishing 20,000 men and persuading Jamuka, a boyhood friend of Temüjin's, to supply an army as well. The contrast between Temüjin's destitution and the huge army furnished by his allies is hard to explain, and no authority other than the narrative of the *Secret History* is available.

RISE TO POWER

With powerful allies and a force of his own, Temüjin routed the Merkit, with the help of a strategy by which Temüjin was regularly to scotch the seeds of future rebellion. He tried never to leave an enemy in his rear; years later, before attacking China, he would first make sure that no nomad leader survived to stab him in the back. Not long after the destruction of the Merkit, he treated the nobility of the Jürkin clan in the same way. These princes, supposedly his allies, had profited by his absence on a raid against the Tatars to plunder his property. Temüjin exterminated the clan nobility and took the common people as his own soldiery and servants. When his power had grown sufficiently for him to risk a final showdown with the formidable Tatars, he first defeated them in battle and then slaughtered all those taller than the height of a cart axle. Presumably the children could be expected to grow up ignorant of their past identity and to become loyal followers of the Mongols. When the alliance with Toghril of the Kereit at last broke down and Temüjin had to dispose of this obstacle to supreme power, he dispersed the Kereit people among the Mongols as servants and troops. This ruthlessness was not mere wanton cruelty. Temüjin intended to leave alive none of the old, rival aristocrats, who might prove a focus of resistance; to provide himself with a fighting force; and, above all, to crush the sense of clan loyalties that favoured fragmentation and to unite all the nomads in personal obedience to his family. And when, in 1206, he was accepted as emperor of all the steppe people, he was to distribute thousands of families to the custody of his own relatives and companions, replacing the existing pattern of tribes and clans by something closer to a feudal structure.

At least from the time of the defeat of the Merkits, Temüjin was aiming at supremacy in the steppes for himself. The renewed friendship with Jamuka lasted only a year and a half. Then, one day while the two friends were on the march, Jamuka uttered an enigmatic remark about the choice of camping site, which provoked Temüjin's wife Börte to advise him that it was high time for the two friends to go their separate ways. What lies behind this episode is difficult to see. The story in the *Secret History* is too puzzling in its brevity and its allusive language to permit a reliable explanation. It has been suggested that Jamuka was trying to provoke a crisis in the leadership. Equally, it may be that the language is deliberately obscure to gloss over the fact that Temüjin was about to desert his comrade. In any event, Temüjin took Börte's advice. Many of Jamuka's own men also abandoned him, probably seeing in Temüjin the man they thought more likely to win in the end. The *Secret History* justifies their action in epic terms. One of the men tells Temüjin of a vision that had appeared to him and that could only be interpreted as meaning that Heaven and Earth had agreed that Temüjin should be lord of the empire. Looking at the situation in a more down-to-earth way, the interplay of the vacillating loyalties of the steppe may be discerned. The clansmen knew what was afoot, and some of them hastened to move over to Temüjin's side, realizing that a strong leader was in the offing and that it would be prudent to declare for him early on.

The break with Jamuka brought about a polarization within the Mongol world that was to be resolved only with the disappearance of one or the other of the rivals. Jamuka has no advocate in history. The *Secret History* has much to tell about him, not always unsympathetically, but it is essentially the chronicle of Temüjin's family; and Jamuka appears as the enemy, albeit sometimes a reluctant one. He is an enigma, a man of sufficient force of personality to lead a rival coalition of princes and to get himself elected *gur-khān*, or supreme khan, by them. Yet he was an intriguer, a man to take the short view, ready to desert his friends, even turn on them, for the sake of a quick profit. But for Temüjin, it might have been within Jamuka's power to dominate the Mongols, but Temüjin was incomparably the greater man; and the rivalry broke Jamuka.

Clan leaders began to group themselves around Temüjin and Jamuka, and, a few years before the turn of the 13th century, some of them proposed to make Temüjin khan of the Mongols. The terms in which they did so, promising him loyalty in war and the hunt, suggest that all they were looking for was a reliable general, certainly not the overlord he was to become. Indeed, later on, some of them were to desert him. Even at this time, Temüjin was only a minor chieftain, as is shown by the next important event narrated by the *Secret History*, a brawl at a feast, provoked by his nominal allies the Jürkin princes, whom he later massacred. The Jin emperor in northern China, too, looked on him as of no great consequence. In one of the reversals of policy characteristic of their manipulation of the nomads, the Jin attacked their onetime allies the Tatars. Together with Toghril, Temüjin seized the opportunity of continuing the clan feud and took the Tatars in the rear. The Jin emperor rewarded Toghril with the Chinese title of *wang*, or prince, and gave Temüjin an even less exalted one. And, indeed, for the next few years the Jin had nothing to fear from Temüjin. He was fully occupied in building up his power in the steppe and posed no obvious threat to China.

Temüjin now set about systematically eliminating all rivals. Successive coalitions formed by Jamuka were defeated. The Tatars were exterminated. Toghril allowed himself to be maneuvered by Jamuka's intrigues and by his own son's ambitions and suspicions into outright war against Temüjin, and he and his Kereit people were destroyed. Finally, in the west, the Naiman ruler, fearful of the rising power of the Mongols, tried to form yet another coalition, with the participation of Jamuka, but was utterly defeated and lost his kingdom. Jamuka, inconstant as ever, deserted the Naiman khan at the last moment. These campaigns took place in the few years before 1206 and left Temüjin master of the steppes. In that year a great assembly was held by the Onon River, and Temüjin was proclaimed Genghis Khan: the title probably meant Universal Ruler.

UNIFICATION OF THE MONGOL NATION

The year 1206 was a turning point in the history of the Mongols and in world history: the moment when the Mongols were first ready to move out beyond the steppe. Mongolia itself took on a new shape. The petty tribal quarrels and raids were a thing of the past. Either the familiar tribe and clan names had fallen out of use or those bearing them were to be found, subsequently, scattered throughout the Mongol world, testifying to the wreck of the traditional clan and tribe system. A unified Mongol nation came into existence as the personal creation of

Genghis Khan and, through many vicissitudes (feudal disintegration, incipient retribalization, colonial occupation), has survived to the present day. Mongol ambitions looked beyond the steppe. Genghis Khan was ready to start on his great adventure of world conquest. The new nation was organized, above all, for war. Genghis Khan's troops were divided up on the decimal system, were rigidly disciplined, and were well equipped and supplied. The generals were his own sons or men he had selected, absolutely loyal to him.

Genghis Khan's military genius could adapt itself to rapidly changing circumstances. Initially his troops were exclusively cavalry, riding the hardy, grass-fed Mongol pony that needed no fodder. With such an army, other nomads could be defeated, but cities could not be taken. Yet before long the Mongols were able to undertake the siege of large cities, using mangonels, catapults, ladders, burning oil, and other methods and even diverting rivers. It was only gradually, through contact with peoples from the more settled states, that Genghis Khan came to realize that there were more sophisticated ways of enjoying power than simply raiding, destroying, and plundering. It was a minister of the khan of the Naiman, the last important Mongol tribe to resist Genghis Khan, who taught him the uses of literacy and helped reduce the Mongol language to writing. The *Secret History* reports it was only after the war against the Muslim empire of Khwārezm, in the region of the Amu Darya (ancient Oxus River) and Syr Darya (ancient Jaxartes River), probably in late 1222, that Genghis Khan learned from Muslim advisers the "meaning and importance of towns." And it was another adviser, formerly in the service of the Jin emperor, who explained to him the uses of peasants and craftsmen as producers of taxable goods. He had intended to turn the cultivated fields of northern China into grazing land for his horses.

The great conquests of the Mongols, which would transform them into a world power, were still to come. China was the main goal. Genghis Khan first secured his western flank by a tough campaign against the Tangut kingdom of Xixia, a northwestern border state of China, and then fell upon the Jin empire of northern China in 1211. In 1214 he allowed himself to be bought off, temporarily, with a huge amount of booty, but in 1215 operations were resumed, and the Jin capital of Zhongdu (present-day Beijing) was taken. Subsequently, the more systematic subjugation of northern China was in the hands of his general Muqali. Genghis Khan himself was compelled to turn aside from China and carry out the conquest of Khwārezm. This war was provoked by the governor of the city of Otrar, who massacred a caravan of Muslim merchants who were under Genghis Khan's protection. The Khwārezm-Shāh refused satisfaction. War with Khwārezm would doubtless have come sooner or later, but now it could not be deferred. It was in this war that the Mongols earned their reputation for savagery and terror. City after city was stormed, the inhabitants massacred or forced to serve as advance troops for the Mongols against their own people. Fields and gardens were laid waste and irrigation works destroyed as Genghis Khan pursued his implacable vengeance against the royal house of Khwārezm. He finally withdrew in 1223 and did not lead his armies into war again until the final campaign against Xixia in 1226–27. He died on August 18, 1227.

ASSESSMENT

As far as can be judged from the disparate sources, Genghis Khan's personality was a complex one. He had great physical strength, tenacity of purpose, and an unbreakable will. He was not obstinate and would listen to advice from others, including his wives and mother. He was flexible. He could deceive but was not petty. He had a sense of the value of loyalty, unlike Toghril or Jamuka. Enemies guilty of treachery toward their lords could expect short shrift from him, but he would exploit their treachery at the same time. He was religiously minded, carried along by his sense of a divine mission, and in moments of crisis he would reverently worship the Eternal Blue Heaven, the supreme deity of the Mongols. So much is true of his early life. The picture becomes less harmonious as he moves out of his familiar sphere and comes into contact with the strange, settled world beyond the steppe. At first he could not see beyond the immediate gains to be got from massacre and rapine and, at times, was consumed by a passion for revenge. Yet all his life he could attract the loyalties of men willing to serve him, both fellow nomads and civilized peoples from the settled world. His fame could even persuade the aged Daoist sage Changchun (Qiu Chuji) to journey the length of Asia to discourse upon religious matters. He was above all adaptable, a man who could learn.

Organization, discipline, mobility, and ruthlessness of purpose were the fundamental factors in his military successes. Massacres of defeated populations, with the resultant terror, were weapons he regularly used. His practice of summoning cities to surrender and of organizing the methodical slaughter of those who did not submit has been described as psychological warfare; but, although it was undoubtedly policy to sap resistance by fostering terror, massacre was used for its own sake. Mongol practice, especially in the war against Khwārezm, was to send agents to demoralize and divide the garrison and populace of an enemy city, mixing threats with promises. The Mongols' reputation for frightfulness often paralyzed their captives, who allowed themselves to be killed when resistance or flight was not impossible. Indeed, the Mongols were unaccountable. Resistance brought certain destruction, but at Balkh, now in Afghanistan, the population was slaughtered in spite of a prompt surrender, for tactical reasons.

The achievements of Genghis Khan were grandiose. He united all the nomadic tribes, and with numerically inferior armies he defeated great empires, such as Khwārezm and the even more powerful Jin state. Yet he did not exhaust his people. He chose his successor, his son Ögödei, with great care, ensured that his other sons would obey Ögödei, and passed on to him an army and a state in full vigour. At the time of his death, Genghis Khan had conquered the land mass extending from Beijing to the Caspian Sea, and his generals had raided Persia and Russia. His successors would extend their power over the whole of China, Persia, and most of Russia. They did what he did not achieve and perhaps never really intended—that is, to weld their conquests into a tightly organized empire. The destruction brought about by Genghis Khan survives in popular memory, but far more significant, these conquests were but the first stage of the Mongol Empire, the greatest continental empire of medieval and modern times.

GIOVANNI DA PIAN DEL CARPINI

(b. c. 1180, Pian del Carpine?, near Perugia, Umbria [Italy]—d. August 1, 1252, Antivari [Bar], Dalmatia?)

The Franciscan friar Giovanni Da Pian Del Carpini (English John of Plano Carpini) was the first noteworthy European traveler in the Mongol Empire, to which he was sent on a formal mission by Pope Innocent IV. He wrote the earliest important Western work on Central Asia.

Giovanni was a contemporary and disciple of St. Francis of Assisi. By 1220 he was a member of the Franciscan order and subsequently became a leading Franciscan teacher in northern Europe; he held successively the offices of custos ("warden") in Saxony and of minister ("subordinate officer") in Germany and afterward in Spain (perhaps also in Barbary and Cologne). He was in Cologne at the time of the great Mongol invasion of eastern Europe and of the disastrous Battle of Liegnitz (April 9, 1241).

Fear of the Mongols had not abated when four years later Pope Innocent IV dispatched the first formal Catholic mission to them, partly to protest against their invasion of Christian territory and partly to gain reliable information about their numbers and their plans; there may also have been the hope of alliance with a power that might be invaluable against Islam. At the head of the mission the Pope placed Giovanni, then already more than 60 years of age.

On Easter Sunday, 1245, Giovanni set out. He was accompanied by Stephen of Bohemia, another friar, who was subsequently to be left behind at Kiev. After seeking counsel of Wenceslaus, king of Bohemia, the friars were joined at Breslau (now Wrocław) by Benedict the Pole, another Franciscan appointed to act as interpreter. The mission entered the Mongol posts at Kanev and thereafter crossed the Dnieper, the Don, and the Volga rivers. On the Volga stood the *ordu*, or "camp," of Batu, the supreme commander on the western frontiers of the Mongol Empire and the conqueror of eastern Europe. Giovanni and his companions, with their presents, had to pass between two fires before being presented to Batu at the beginning of April 1246. Batu ordered them to proceed to the court of the supreme khan in Mongolia, and accordingly, on Easter day, April 8, 1246, they began the second and more formidable part of their journey. Their bodies were tightly bandaged to enable them to endure the excessive fatigue of their great ride through Central Asia. Their route was across the Ural (Yaik) River and north of the Caspian Sea and the Aral Sea to the Syr Darya (ancient Jaxartes River) and the Muslim cities, which then stood on its banks, then along the shores of the Dzungarian lakes and thence to the imperial camp of Sira Ordu (i.e., the "yellow pavilion") near Karakorum and the Orkhon River. They reached their destination on July 22, after a ride of about 3,000 miles (5,000 km) in just over 106 days.

On arriving at Sira Ordu, the Franciscans found that the interregnum that had followed the death of Ögödei, the supreme khan, or imperial ruler, had ended. His eldest son, Güyük (Kuyug), had been designated to the throne; his formal election in a great *kuriltai*, or general assembly of shamans, was witnessed by the friars along with more than 3,000 envoys and deputies from all parts of the Mongol Empire. On August 24 they were present at the formal enthronement at the nearby camp of the "Golden" Ordu and were presented to the supreme khan. They were detained until November and were then dismissed with a letter for the Pope, which was little more than a brief imperious assertion of the khan's role as the scourge of God. The friars suffered greatly on their long winter journey homeward, and not until June 9, 1247, did they reach Kiev, where they were welcomed by the Slavic Christians as risen from the dead. Subsequently they delivered the khan's letter and made their report to the pope, who was still at Lyon.

Immediately after his return, Giovanni recorded his observations in a large work variously styled in the manuscripts extant as *Historia Mongalorum quos nos Tartaros appellamus* ("History of the Mongols Whom We Call the Tartars") and *Liber Tartarorum* ("Book of the Tartars"), or *Tatarorum*. He divided his treatise into eight chapters on the country of the Mongols, their climate, customs, religion, character, history, policy and tactics, and on the best way of resisting them; in a ninth chapter he described the regions traversed. He added four name lists: of the peoples conquered by the Mongols, of those who had successfully to his time (1245–47) remained unconquered, of the Mongol princes, and of witnesses to the truth of his *Historia*, including several merchants trading in Kiev. His *Historia* discredited the many fables concerning the Mongols current in Western Christendom. Its account of Mongol customs and history is probably the best treatment of the subject by any medieval Christian writer, and only on geographical and personal detail is it inferior to one written a few years later by the papal envoy to the Mongols Willem Van Ruysbroeck (William of Rubrouck). Giovanni's companion, Benedict the Pole, also left a brief account of the mission, taken down from his dictation. Not long after his return, Giovanni was installed as archbishop of Antivari in Dalmatia and was sent as legate to Louis IX.

For a long time the *Historia* was only partially known through an abstract in the great compendium of Vincent of Beauvais (*Speculum historiale*), made a generation after Giovanni's own and first printed in 1473. Richard Hakluyt (1598) and P. Bergeron (1634) published portions of the text, but the complete work was not printed until 1839: M.A.P. d'Avezac (ed.) in *Recueil de voyages et de mémoires*, vol. 4, Geographical Society of Paris.

WILLEM VAN RUYSBROECK

(b. c. 1215—d. c. 1295)

Willem Van Ruysbroeck (Latin Wilhelmus Rubruquis, English William of Rubrouck) was a French Franciscan friar whose eyewitness account of the Mongol realm is generally acknowledged to be the best written by any medieval Christian traveler. A contemporary of the English scientist and philosopher Roger Bacon, he was cited frequently in the geographical section of Bacon's *Opus majus*.

Willem was probably from the village of Rubrouck, near Saint-Omer, France. In 1253 King Louis IX of France (St. Louis), who was then at Acre, Palestine, dispatched him on an informal mission to the Mongol Empire. Departing from Constantinople (modern Istanbul) on May 7, 1253, he and his party reached the Crimean town of Sudak. There they secured oxen and carts for their long trek across the steppes to the encampment of Batu Khan, the Mongol ruler of the Volga River region. Following their arrival five weeks later, they were ordered to begin a journey of some 5,000 miles (8,000 km) to the court of the Great Khan at Karakorum in central Mongolia.

The Christians set off on horseback on September 16, 1253, their route taking them north of the Caspian and Aral seas to the Talas River, to the Cailac Valley, and to the great plains of Mongolia, and came upon the Great Khan's camp, which lay about 10 days' journey south of Karakorum. Willem and his companions were received

A brick relief image depicting Willem Van Ruysbroeck on horseback. © Hemis.fr/SuperStock

courteously and remained with the Khan until about July 10, 1254. They followed a more northerly route on their outward journey, reaching Tripoli on August 15, 1255, where they found that King Louis had returned to France in 1254.

Willem wrote about his Mongolian experiences for the French king. His narrative is free from legend and shows him to have been an intelligent and honest observer. Nothing is known about his later life, except that he was alive when Marco Polo returned from the East in 1295. After Bacon's copious use of the narrative, it was neglected, though five manuscripts survive. One copy was imperfectly reproduced by Richard Hakluyt in 1598 and 1599. A much later Hakluyt Society edition is *The Journey of William of Rubruck to the Eastern Parts of the World, 1253–55...* (1900), prepared by W.W. Rockhill.

GIOVANNI DA MONTECORVINO

(b. 1247, Montecorvino, Sicily [Italy]—d. 1328, Dadu [now Beijing], China)

Giovanni da Montecorvino was an Italian Franciscan missionary who founded the earliest Roman Catholic missions in India and China and became the first archbishop of Dadu (modern Beijing).

In 1272 Montecorvino was commissioned by the Byzantine emperor Michael VIII Palaeologus as an emissary to Pope Gregory X to negotiate the reunion of Greek and Roman churches. He began his missionary work in Armenia and Persia about 1280. In 1289 Pope Nicholas IV sent him as emissary to the Il-Khan of Persia. From Tabriz, then the chief city of western Asia, Montecorvino moved down to the Madras region of southern India, from which he wrote (1292/93) the earliest noteworthy Western account of that region of the Indian seaboard known historically as the Coromandel Coast. In 1294 he entered the Yuan (Mongol) capital of Dadu (Beijing). His letters of 1305 and 1306 describe the progress of the Roman mission in the Far East—including opposition by the Nestorian Christians—and allude to the Roman Catholic community he had founded in India.

In 1307 Pope Clement V created him archbishop of Dadu and patriarch of the Orient and to consecrate and assist him sent seven bishops, only three of whom survived the journey. A Franciscan tradition maintains that in 1311 Montecorvino baptized the Yuan emperor Khaishan (Güiük; ruled 1307–11) and his mother. This event has been disputed, but he was unquestionably successful in northern and eastern China. He was apparently the only effective European proselytizer in medieval Beijing, but the results of his mission were lost in the downfall of the Yuan dynasty during the 14th century.

MARCO POLO

(b. c. 1254, Venice [Italy]—d. January 8, 1324, Venice)

The Venetian merchant and adventurer Marco Polo traveled from Europe to Asia in 1271–95, remaining in China for 17 of those years. His *Il milione* ("The Million"), known in English as the *Travels of Marco Polo*, is a classic of travel literature.

TRAVELS OF THE POLO FAMILY

Polo's way was paved by the pioneering efforts of his ancestors, especially his father, Niccolò, and his uncle, Maffeo. The family had traded with the Middle East for a long time, acquiring considerable wealth and prestige. Although it is uncertain if the Polos were of the nobility, the matter was of little importance in Venice, a city of republican and mercantile traditions.

The family appears to have been shrewd, alert, and courageous; about 1260 they foresaw a political change in Constantinople (modern Istanbul)—e.g., the overthrow of the Crusaders who had ruled since 1204 by Michael VIII Palaeologus in 1261—and liquidated their property there, invested their capital in jewels, and set off for the Volga River, where Berke Khan, sovereign of the western territories in the Mongol Empire, held court at Sarai or Bulgar. The Polos apparently managed their affairs well at Berke's court, where they doubled their assets. When political events prevented their return to Venice, they traveled eastward to Bukhara (Bokhara) and ended their journey in 1265, probably at the grand khan's summer residence, Shangdu (immortalized as Xanadu by English poet Samuel Taylor Coleridge). Establishing friendly relations with the great Kublai Khan, they eventually returned to Europe as his ambassadors, carrying letters asking the pope to send Kublai 100 intelligent men "acquainted with the Seven Arts"; they also bore gifts and were asked to bring back oil from the lamp burning at the Holy Sepulchre in Jerusalem.

POLO'S JOURNEY TO ASIA

Little is known about Marco's early years except that he probably grew up in Venice. He was age 15 or 16 when his father and uncle returned to meet him and learned that the pope, Clement IV, had recently died. Niccolò and Maffeo remained in Venice anticipating the election of a new pope, but in 1271, after two years of waiting, they departed with Marco for the Mongol court. In Acre (now ʿAkko, Israel) the papal legate, Teobaldo of Piacenza, gave them letters for the Mongol emperor. The Polos had been on the road for only a few days when they heard that their friend Teobaldo had been elected pope as Gregory X. Returning to Acre, they were given proper credentials, and two friars were assigned to accompany them, though they abandoned the Polos shortly after the expedition resumed.

From Acre the travelers proceeded to Ayas ("Laiazzo" in Marco's writings, now Yumurtalik, on the Gulf of İskenderun, also called the Gulf of Alexandretta, in south-eastern Turkey). During the early part of 1272, they probably passed through Erzurum, in what is now eastern Turkey, and Tabriz, in what is now northern Iran, later crossing inhospitable deserts infested with brigands before reaching Hormuz on the Persian Gulf. There the Polos decided not to risk a sea passage to India and beyond but to proceed overland to the Mongol capital.

They next traveled through deserts of "surpassing aridity" toward the Khorasan region in what is now eastern Iran. Turning gradually to the northeast, they reached more hospitable lands; Badakhshān ("Balascian"), in Afghanistan, in particular, pleased the travelers. Marco suggests that they remained there for a year; detained, perhaps, by illness (possibly malaria) that was cured by the benign climate of the district. It is also believed that Marco visited territories to the south (other parts of Afghanistan, Kafiristan in the Hindu Kush, Chitral in what is now Pakistan, and perhaps Kashmir) during this period. It is, however, difficult to establish which districts he traversed and which he may have described from information gathered en route.

Commemorative medal depicting the image of the Venetian merchant and adventurer Marco Polo. Universal Images Group/Getty Images

Leaving Badakhshān, the Polos proceeded toward the Pamirs, but the route they followed to cross these Central Asian highlands remains uncertain. Descending on the northeastern side of the chain, they reached Kashi ("Cascar") in what is now the Uygur Autonomous Region of Xinjiang, China. By this point the Polos were on the main Silk Road, and they probably followed along the oases to the south and east of the Takla Makan Desert—Yarkant ("Yarcan"), Hotan ("Cotan"), Che'erchen ("Ciarcian"), and Lop Nur (Lop Lake).

These stepping-stones led to Shazhou ("Saciu") on the borders of China, a place now called Dunhuang.

Before reaching Shazhou, the Polos had traveled primarily among Muslim peoples, though they also encountered Nestorian Christians, Buddhists, Manichaeans, and Zoroastrians. In the vast province of Gansu (called "Tangut" by Marco), an entirely different civilization—mainly Buddhist in religion but partly Chinese in culture— prevailed. The travelers probably stopped in Suzhou ("Sukchu"; now Jiuquan) and Ganzhou ("Campiciu"; now Zhangye) before entering the Ningxia area. It is not clear whether they reached the Mongol summer capital of Shangdu ("Ciandu") directly or after a detour; in any event, sometime in 1275 (1274, according to the research of Japanese scholar Matsuo Otagi) the Polos were again at the Mongol court, presenting the sacred oil from Jerusalem and the papal letters to their patron, Kublai Khan.

SOJOURN IN CHINA

For the next 16 or 17 years the Polos lived in the emperor's dominions, which included, among other places, Cathay (now North China) and Mangi, or "Manzi" (now South China). They may have moved with the court from Shangdu, to the winter residence, Dadu, or "Taidu" (modern Beijing).

Unfortunately, because Marco's book *Il milione* is only incidentally a biography and autobiography, it is exceedingly difficult to ascertain where the Polos went and what they did during these years. Nevertheless, it is well known that many foreigners were in the employ of the state, since the Mongol rulers did not trust their Chinese subjects; so it would have been natural for the Polos to fit in most honourably and successfully with this motley society.

The extent of their success and the specific roles they filled, however, remains an open question. The elder Polos were probably employed in some technical capacity. Once and very abruptly, a glimpse in *Il milione* is obtained of them acting as military advisers during the siege of "Saianfu" (formerly Xiangyang, now Xiangfan), a city that was finally taken, according to Marco, thanks to some "great mangonels" (missile-throwing engines) built according to the Polos' specifications. The whole episode is dubious, however.

Marco was about age 20 when he reached Cathay. Although he knew little or no Chinese, he did speak some of the many languages then used in East Asia—most probably Turkish (in its Coman dialect) as spoken among the Mongols, Arabized Persian, Uighur (Uygur), and perhaps Mongol. He was noticed very favourably by Kublai, who took great delight in hearing of strange countries and repeatedly sent him on fact-finding missions to distant parts of the empire. One such journey took Polo to Yunnan in southwestern China and perhaps as far as Tagaung in Myanmar (Burma); on another occasion he visited southeastern China, later enthusiastically describing the city of "Quinsay" (now Hangzhou) and the populous regions recently conquered by the Mongols. Apart from the missions he undertook for the emperor, Polo may have held other administrative responsibilities, including inspection of the customs duties and revenues collected from the trade in salt and other commodities. According to some versions of *Il milione*, he governed the city of Yangzhou for three years sometime between 1282 and 1287; but this assertion seems hardly credible and hinges entirely on the interpretation of one word. There is, however, ample evidence to show that Polo considered himself an adoptive son of his new country.

THE RETURN TO VENICE

Sometime around 1292 (1290 according to Otagi), a Mongol princess was to be sent to Persia to become the consort of Arghun Khan, and the Polos offered to accompany her. Marco wrote that Kublai had been unwilling to let them go but finally granted permission. They were eager to leave, in part, because Kublai was nearly 80, and his death (and the consequent change in regime) might have been dangerous for a small group of isolated foreigners. Naturally, they also longed to see their native Venice and their families again.

The princess, with some 600 courtiers and sailors, and the Polos boarded 14 ships, which left the port of Quanzhou ("Zaiton") and sailed southward. The fleet stopped briefly at Champa ("Ciamba," modern Vietnam) as well as a number of islands and the Malay Peninsula before settling for five months on the island of Sumatra ("Lesser Giaua") to avoid monsoon storms. There Polo was much impressed by the fact that the North Star appeared to have dipped below the horizon. The fleet then passed near the Nicobar Islands ("Necuveran"), touched land again in Sri Lanka, or Ceylon ("Seilan"), followed the west coast of India and the southern reaches of Persia, and finally anchored at Hormuz. The expedition then proceeded to Khorasan, handing over the princess not to Arghun, who had died, but to his son Maḥmūd Ghāzān.

The Polos eventually departed for Europe, but their movements at this point are unclear; possibly they stayed for a few months in Tabriz. Unfortunately, as soon as they left the Mongol dominions and set foot in a Christian country, at Trebizond in what is now Turkey, they were robbed of most of their hard-won earnings. After further delays, they reached Constantinople and finally Venice (1295). The story of their dramatic recognition by relatives and neighbours who had thought them long since dead is a part of Polo lore that is well known.

COMPILATION OF *IL MILIONE*

Soon after his return to Venice, Polo was taken prisoner by the Genoese—great rivals of the Venetians at sea—during a skirmish or battle in the Mediterranean. He was then imprisoned in Genoa, where he had a felicitous encounter with a prisoner from Pisa, Rustichello (or Rusticiano), a fairly well-known writer of romances and a specialist in chivalry and its lore, then a fashionable subject. Polo may have intended to write about his 25 years in Asia but possibly did not feel sufficiently comfortable in either Venetian or Franco-Italian; however, with Rustichello at hand, the traveler began dictating his tale. The language employed was Franco-Italian—a strange composite tongue fashionable during the 13th and 14th centuries.

Polo was soon freed and returned to Venice. The remainder of his life can be reconstructed, in part, through the testimony of legal documents. He seems to have led a quiet existence, managing a not too conspicuous fortune and dying at age 70. His will set free a "Tatar slave" who may possibly have followed him from East Asia. A famous story relates how Polo was asked on his deathbed to retract the "fables" he had invented in his book; his answer was that he told barely half of what he actually saw.

NATURE AND CONTENT OF *IL MILIONE*

An instant success—"In a few months it spread throughout Italy," wrote Giovanni Battista Ramusio, the 16th-century

Italian geographer—*Il milione* was apparently conceived as a vast cosmography based on firsthand experience. The book was not intended to be a collection of personal recollections, which leaves Polo's own personality somewhat elusive, but *Divisament dou monde* ("Description of the World"), as it was originally titled, was to be the book to end all books on Asia. Nonetheless, details concerning travel, distances covered, and seasons are rarely stated; the panorama is observed from an impersonal distance with a powerful wide-angle lens. In *Il milione* Polo often branches off into descriptions of places probably visited not by himself but by his relatives or people he knew. Typical digressions are those on Mesopotamia, the Assassins and their castles, Samarkand, Siberia, Japan, India, Ethiopia, and Madagascar. *Il milione* is better understood not as biography but as part of the vernacular didactic literature, of which the Middle Ages offer many examples.

The work is marked by uncertainty and controversy, however. The origin of the popular title, *Il milione*, for example, is not quite clear. Although it most likely comes from Polo's nickname, Il Milione, from his tendency to describe the millions of things he saw in the Mongol Empire, it may have been related to the idea of a "tall story," or from a nickname running in the family, possibly traceable to a corruption of Aemilione ("Big Emil"). The history of the text itself is characterized by similar uncertainty. There is no authentic original manuscript, and even if there were, it would likely not represent what Polo dictated since Rustichello asserted his own personality and familiar phraseology, especially in the standardized description of battles. Polo also seems to have made emendations himself on various copies of the work during the last 20 years or so of his life. Some editors—for instance, the friar Pipino, who made a good Latin translation of the original—found many of Polo's descriptions or interpretations impious or dangerously near to heresy and therefore heavily bowdlerized the text. Furthermore, since all this happened long before the invention of printing, professional scribes or amateurs made dozens of copies of the book, as well as free translations and adaptations—often adding to or subtracting from the text with little or no respect for authenticity. There were many unfamiliar names that rarely passed unchanged from one copy to another. Consequently, there are some 140 different manuscript versions of the text in three manuscript groups, in a dozen different languages and dialects—an immensely complex and controversial body of material representing one of the most obdurate philological problems inherited from the Middle Ages.

SUBSEQUENT REPUTATION

As a result of Polo's reticence concerning personal matters and the controversies surrounding the text, Polo's reputation has suffered dramatic ups and downs. For some scholars, novelists, filmmakers, and dramatists, he was a brilliant young courtier, a man of prodigious memory, a most conscientious observer, and a successful official at the cosmopolitan court of the Mongol rulers. For others he was a braggart, a drifter ready to believe the gossip of ports and bazaars, a man with little culture, scant imagination, and a total lack of humour. Still others argue that he never went to China at all, noting that he failed, among other things, to mention the Great Wall of China, the use of tea, and the ideographic script of the Far East, and that contemporary Chinese records show no trace of Polo. (But under what name was he known? Who would recognize the 16th- and 17th-century Italian missionary Matteo Ricci under Li Matou or the 18th-century painter Giuseppe Castiglione under Lang Shining?)

A more balanced view must take into account many factors, especially the textual problem and medieval ideas of the world. Modern scholarship and research have, however, given a new depth and scope to his work. It is generally recognized that he reported faithfully what he saw and heard, but that much of what he heard was fabulous or distorted. In any case, Polo's account opened new vistas to the European mind, and as Western horizons expanded, Polo's influence grew as well. His description of Japan set a definite goal for Christopher Columbus in his journey in 1492, while his detailed localizations of spices encouraged Western merchants to seek out these areas and break the age-old Arab trading monopoly. The wealth of new geographic information recorded by Polo was widely used in the late 15th and the 16th centuries, during the age of the great European voyages of discovery and conquest.

ODORIC OF PORDENONE

(b. c. 1286, Villanova, near Pordenone, Aquileia [Italy]—d. January 14, 1331, Udine)

Odoric of Pordenone was a Franciscan friar and traveler, whose account of his journey to China enjoyed wide popularity and appears to have been plagiarized in the 14th-century English work *The Voyage and Travels of Sir John Mandeville, Knight*, generally known as *Mandeville's Travels*.

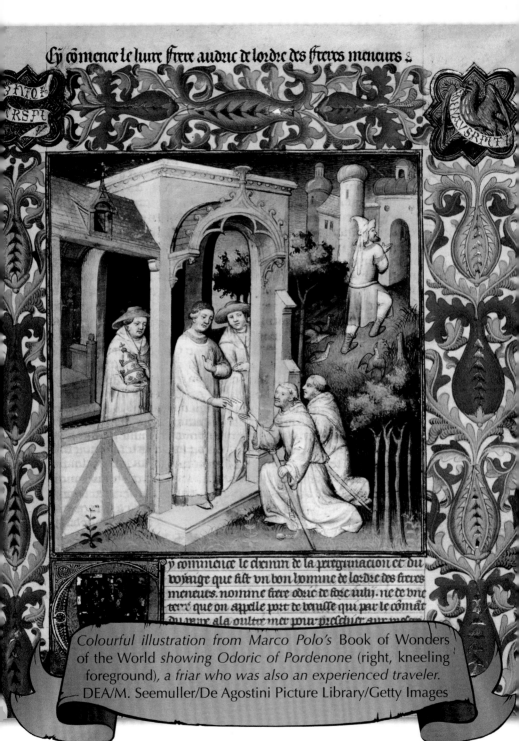

Colourful illustration from Marco Polo's Book of Wonders of the World *showing Odoric of Pordenone (right, kneeling foreground), a friar who was also an experienced traveler.* DEA/M. Seemuller/De Agostini Picture Library/Getty Images

After taking his vows at Udine, Odoric was sent to Asia (*c.* 1316–18), where he remained until 1329. Passing through Asia Minor, he visited Franciscan houses at Trabzon and Erzurum, now in Turkey. He circled through Persia, stopping at the Franciscan house at Tabriz and continuing on to Kashan, Yazd, Persepolis, and Shīrāz before touring the Baghdad region of Mesopotamia. He then went to Hormuz (now in Iran) at the southern end of the Persian Gulf and eventually embarked for India.

After landing at Thana, near present-day Mumbai (Bombay), about 1322, Odoric visited many parts of India and possibly Ceylon (now Sri Lanka). He sailed in a junk for the north coast of Sumatra, touching on Java and perhaps Borneo before reaching the south China coast. He traveled extensively in China and visited Hang-chou (Hangzhou), renowned as the greatest city in the world, whose splendour he described in detail. After three years at Beijing, he set out for home, probably by way of Tibet (including Lhasa) and northern Persia. By the time he reached Italy, he had baptized more than 20,000 persons. At Padua the story of his travels was taken down in simple Latin by another friar. Several months later Odoric died while on the way to the papal court at Avignon.

The story of his journeys seems to have made a greater impression on the laity of Udine than on Odoric's Franciscan brethren. The latter were about to bury him when the chief magistrate (*gastaldi*) of the city interfered and ordered a public funeral. Popular acclamation made Odoric an object of devotion, and the municipality erected a shrine for his body. Although his fame was widespread before the middle of the 14th century, he was not formally beatified until 1755.

IBN BAṬṬŪṬAH

(b. February 24, 1304, Tangier, Morocco—d.
1368/69 or 1377, Morocco)

Abū ʿAbd Allāh Muḥammad ibn ʿAbd Allāh al-Lawātī al-Ṭanjī ibn Baṭṭūṭah was not only the greatest medieval Arab traveler but also the author of one of the world's most famous travel books, the *Riḥlah* (*Travels*), which describes his extensive travels covering some 75,000 miles (more than 120,000 km) in trips to almost all the Muslim countries and as far as China and the island of Sumatra.

LIFE AND TRAVELS

Ibn Baṭṭūṭah was from a family that produced a number of Muslim judges (*qāḍīs*). He received the traditional juristic and literary education in his native town of Tangier. In 1325, at the age of 21, he started his travels by undertaking the pilgrimage to Mecca. At first his purpose was to fulfill this religious duty and to broaden his education by studying under famous scholars in the Middle East (Egypt, Syria, and the Hejaz). That he achieved his objectives is corroborated by long enumerations of scholars and Sufi (Islamic mystic) saints whom he met and also by a list of diplomas conferred upon him (mainly in Damascus). These studies qualified him for judicial office, whereas the claim of being a former pupil of the then-outstanding authorities in traditional Islamic sciences greatly enhanced his chances and made him thereafter a respected guest at many courts.

But this was to follow later. In Egypt, where he arrived by the land route along the North African coast via Tunis and Tripoli, an irresistible passion for travel was born in his soul, and he decided to visit as many parts of the world as possible, setting as a rule "never to travel any road a second time." His contemporaries traveled for practical reasons (such as trade, pilgrimage, and education), but Ibn Baṭṭūṭah did it for its own sake, for the joy of learning about new countries and new peoples. He made a living of it, benefitting at the beginning from his scholarly status and later from his increasing fame as a traveler. He enjoyed the generosity and benevolence of numerous sultans, rulers, governors, and high dignitaries in the countries he visited, thus securing an income that enabled him to continue his wanderings.

From Cairo, Ibn Baṭṭūṭah set out via Upper Egypt to the Red Sea but then returned and visited Syria, there joining a caravan for Mecca. Having finished the pilgrimage in 1326, he crossed the Arabian Desert to Iraq, southern Iran, Azerbaijan, and Baghdad. There he met the last of the Mongol khans of Iran, Abū Saʿīd (ruled 1316–36), and some lesser rulers. Ibn Baṭṭūṭah spent the years between 1327 and 1330 in Mecca and Medina leading the quiet life of a devotee, but such a long stay did not suit his temperament.

Embarking on a boat in Jiddah, he sailed with a retinue of followers down both shores of the Red Sea to Yemen, crossed it by land, and set sail again from Aden. This time he navigated along the eastern African coast, visiting the trading city-states as far as Kilwa (now in Tanzania). His return journey took him to southern Arabia, Oman,

Arab traveler Ibn Baṭṭūṭah, viewing ancient ruins in Egypt.
Universal Images Group/Getty Images

Hormuz, southern Persia, and across the Persian Gulf back to Mecca in 1332.

There a new, ambitious plan matured in his mind. Hearing of the sultan of Delhi, Muḥammad ibn Tughluq (ruled 1325–51), and his fabulous generosity to Muslim scholars, he decided to try his luck at his court. Forced by lack of communications to choose a more indirect route, Ibn Baṭṭūṭah turned northward, again passed Egypt and Syria, and boarded ship for Asia Minor (Anatolia) in Latakia. He crisscrossed this "land of the Turks" in many directions at a time when that region was divided into numerous petty sultanates. Thus, his narrative provides a valuable source for the history of this country between the end of the Seljuq power and the rise of the house of Ottoman. Ibn Baṭṭūṭah was received cordially and generously by all the local rulers and heads of religious brotherhoods (akhīs).

His journey continued across the Black Sea to the Crimea, then to the northern Caucasus and to Saray on the lower Volga, capital of the khan of the Golden Horde, Muḥammad Özbeg (ruled 1312–41). According to his narrative, he undertook an excursion from Saray to Bulgary on the upper Volga and Kama rivers, but there are reasons to doubt his veracity on this point. On the other hand, the narrative of his visit to Constantinople (modern Istanbul) in the retinue of the khan's wife, a Byzantine princess, seems to be an eyewitness record, although there are some minor chronological discrepancies. Ibn Baṭṭūṭah's description of the Byzantine capital is vivid and, in general, accurate. Although he shared the strong opinions of his fellow Muslims toward unbelievers, his account of the "second Rome" shows him as a rather tolerant man with a lively curiosity. Nevertheless, he always felt happier in the realm of Islam than in non-Muslim lands, whether Christian, Hindu, or pagan.

After his return from Constantinople through the Russian steppes, he continued his journey in the general direction of India. From Saray he traveled with a caravan to Central Asia, visiting the ancient towns of Bukhara, Samarkand, and Balkh, all of these still showing the scars left by the Mongol invasion. He took rather complicated routes through Khorāsān and Afghanistan, and, after crossing the Hindu Kush (mountains), he arrived at the frontiers of India on the Indus River on September 12, 1333, by his own dating. The accuracy of this date is doubtful, as it would have been impossible to cover such enormous distances (from Mecca) in the course of only one year. Because of this discrepancy, his subsequent dating until 1348 is highly uncertain.

At this time he was already a man of some importance and fame, with a large train of attendants and followers and also with his own harem of legal wives and concubines. India and its ruler, Muḥammad ibn Tughluq, lived up to Ibn Baṭṭūṭah's expectations of wealth and generosity, and the traveler was received with honours and gifts and later appointed grand *qāḍī* of Delhi, a sinecure that he held for several years.

Though he had apparently attained an easy life, it soon became clear that his new position was not without danger. Sultan Muḥammad, an extraordinary mixture of generosity and cruelty, held sway over the greater part of India with an iron hand that fell indiscriminately upon high and low, Muslim and Hindu alike. Ibn Baṭṭūṭah witnessed all the glories and setbacks of the sultan and his rule, fearing daily for his life as he saw many friends fall victim to the suspicious despot. His portrait of Muḥammad is an unusually fine piece of psychological insight and mirrors faithfully the author's mixed feelings of terror and sympathy. Notwithstanding all his precautions, Ibn Baṭṭūṭah at last fell into disgrace, and only good fortune saved his life;

gaining favour again, he was appointed the sultan's envoy to the Chinese emperor in 1342.

He left Delhi without regrets, but his journey was full of other dangers: not far away from Delhi his party was waylaid by Hindu insurgents, and the traveler barely escaped with his life. On the Malabar Coast he became involved in local wars and was finally shipwrecked near Calicut (now Kozhikode), losing all his property and the presents for the Chinese emperor. Fearing the wrath of the sultan, Ibn Baṭṭūṭah chose to go to the Maldive Islands, where he spent nearly two years; as a *qāḍī*, he was soon active in politics, married into the ruling family, and apparently even aspired to become sultan.

Finding the situation too dangerous, he set out for Ceylon (Sri Lanka), where he visited the ruler as well as the famous Adam's Peak. After a new shipwreck on the Coromandel Coast, of eastern India, he took part in a war led by his brother-in-law and went again to the Maldives and then to Bengal and Assam. At this time he decided to resume his mission to China and sailed for Sumatra. There he was given a new ship by the Muslim sultan and started for China; his description of his itinerary contains some discrepancies.

He landed at the great Chinese port Zaytūn (identified as Quanzhou, near Xiamen [Amoy]) and then traveled on inland waterways as far as Dadu (now Beijing) and back. This part of his narrative is rather brief, and the itinerary, as well as the chronology, presents many problems and difficulties, not yet surmounted, that cast shadows of doubt on his veracity.

Equally brief is his account of the return voyage via Sumatra, Malabar, and the Persian Gulf to Baghdad and Syria. In Syria he witnessed the ravages of the Black Death of 1348, visited again many towns there and in Egypt, and in the same year performed his final pilgrimage to Mecca.

At last he decided to return home, sailing from Alexandria to Tunisia, then to Sardinia and Algiers, finally reaching Fès, the capital of the Marīnid sultan, Abū ʿInān, in November 1349.

But there still remained two Muslim countries not yet known to him. Shortly after his return he went to the kingdom of Granada, the last remnant of Moorish Spain, and two years later (in 1352) he set out on a journey to the western Sudan. His last journey (across the Sahara to Western Africa) was taken unwillingly at the command of the sultan. Crossing the Sahara, he spent a year in the empire of Mali, then at the height of its power under Mansa Sulaymān; his account represents one of the most important sources of that period for the history of that part of Africa.

Toward the end of 1353 Ibn Baṭṭūṭah returned to Morocco and, at the sultan's request, dictated his reminiscences to a writer, Ibn Juzayy (died 1355), who embellished the simple prose of Ibn Baṭṭūṭah with an ornate style and fragments of poetry. After that he passes from sight. He is reported to have held the office of *qāḍī* in a town in Morocco before his death, details of which remain uncertain. It has been suggested that he died in 1368/69 or 1377 and was buried in his native town of Tangier.

ASSESSMENT

The claim of Ibn Baṭṭūṭah to be "the traveler of Islam" is well founded: it is estimated that the extent of his wanderings was some 75,000 miles (120,000 km), a figure hardly surpassed by anyone before the age of steam. He visited, with few exceptions (central Persia, Armenia, and Georgia), all Muslim countries, as well as many adjacent non-Muslim lands. While he did not discover new or unknown lands, and his contribution to scientific geography was minimal, the documentary value of his work has given it lasting historical and geographical significance. He met at least 60 rulers and a much greater number of viziers, governors, and other dignitaries; in his book he mentioned more than 2,000 persons who were known to him personally or whose tombs he visited. The majority of these people are identifiable by independent sources, and there are surprisingly few errors in names or dates in Ibn Baṭṭūṭah's material.

His *Riḥlah*, as his book is commonly known, is an important document shedding light on many aspects of the social, cultural, and political history of a great part of the Muslim world. A curious observer interested in the ways of life in various countries, he describes his experiences with a human approach rarely encountered in official historiography. His accounts of his travels in Asia Minor, East and West Africa, the Maldives, and India form a major source for the histories of these areas, whereas the parts dealing with the Arab and Persian Middle East are valuable for their wealth of detail on various aspects of social and cultural life.

On the whole, Ibn Baṭṭūṭah is reliable; only his alleged journey to Bulgary was proved to be invented, and there are some doubts concerning the East Asian part of his travels. A few grave and several minor discrepancies in the chronology of his travels are due more to lapses in his memory than to intentional fabrication. A number of formerly uncertain points (such as travels in Asia Minor and the visit to Constantinople) have since been cleared away by contemporary research and the discovery of new corroborative sources.

Another interesting aspect of the *Riḥlah* is the gradual revealing of the character of Ibn Baṭṭūṭah himself; in the course of the narrative the reader may learn the opinions and reactions of an average middle-class Muslim of the 14th century. He was deeply rooted in orthodox Islam but, like many of his contemporaries, oscillated between the pursuit of its legislative formalism and an adherence to the mystic path and succeeded in combining both. He did not offer any profound philosophy but accepted life as it came to him, leaving to posterity a true picture of himself and his times.

CONCLUSION

I t is now widely believed that a very long time ago the earliest humans spread throughout and inhabited the Old World and eventually reached the New. There is little to suggest, however, that for tens of thousands of years the people inhabiting Asia, Europe, and the Americas had much, if any, contact with others outside of the relatively limited geographic areas where they lived. Undoubtedly, the rise of agriculture, animal husbandry, specialized occupations, and cities were instrumental in paving the way for those curious about what lay beyond the familiar and known world.

It is not certain when people began traveling widely away from their homelands and then returning to them. The archaeological record and earliest historical documents indicate that sometime between 3,000 and 4,000 years ago peoples such as the Phoenicians in the Mediterranean, the Egyptians in the Middle East, the Lapita in the South Pacific, and the Celts in much of Europe started to venture increasingly greater distances as conquerors, colonizers, and traders. As technology in transportation and warfare advanced, men of high ambition, such as Alexander the Great, Julius Caesar, and Genghis Khan, were able to take and subjugate vast regions of Europe and Asia far beyond their native lands, combining a desire for empire building with an urge to seek out new places and people. Others, such as the Norse, sailed to faraway places across the ocean to establish remote outposts.

Increasingly, individuals also set forth on journeys in ancient times seeking economic opportunities, religious convictions, personal glory, or, simply, a spirit of discovery and adventure. Most of these people were Europeans—perhaps best represented by Marco Polo—but others, such as the Chinese explorer Zhang Qian and the Muslim traveler Ibn Baṭṭūṭah, were instrumental in expanding the horizons of the Han dynasty and the Islamic world, respectively. Of great importance were the writings that many of these people left behind. Often these books were rife with inaccuracies, misrepresentations, and exaggerations. Yet the documents also contained much that was true in their vivid descriptions and stories of exotic otherworldly places, cultures, and customs. These accounts fired the imaginations of those who read them and contributed to a growing desire to see these lands, as well as those yet undiscovered. What followed in Europe in the 15th and first half of the 16th centuries was the era now known as the great age of exploration.

GLOSSARY

caliph A Muslim title used when referring to a successor of Muhammad as temporal and spiritual head of Islam.

chert A rock resembling flint.

consort A ship that accompanies another in a sailing expedition.

druid One of an ancient Celtic priesthood, appearing in Irish and Welsh sagas and Christian legends as magicians and wizards.

fountainhead The principal or original source.

interregnum The time during which a throne is vacant between two successive reigns or regimes.

isthmus A narrow strip of land connecting two larger land areas.

nomad A member of a people who have no fixed residence but move from place to place, usually seasonally and within a well-defined territory.

obsidian A dark natural glass formed by the cooling of molten lava.

phalanx A body of heavily armed infantry in ancient Greece formed in close deep ranks and files.

pharaoh An ancient-Egyptian ruler.

potentate A ruler with great power to control or sway his subjects.

quell To quiet or reduce to submission.

regalia The trappings of royalty, including emblems, symbols, and paraphernalia.

renegade A deserter from one faith, cause, or allegiance to another.

satraps Governors of ancient-Persian provinces.

subjugate To bring under control and governance as a subject.

sutra One of the discourses of the Buddha that constitute the basic text of Buddhist scripture

suzerain A superior feudal lord to whom fealty is due; also called an overlord.

BIBLIOGRAPHY

Two general works are *Aedeen Cremin, The World Encyclopedia of Archaeology: The World's Most Significant Sites and Treasures* (2007); and Mauricio Obregón, *Beyond the Edge of the Sea: Sailing with Jason and the Argonauts, Ulysses, the Vikings, and Other Explorers of the Ancient World* (2001). Useful studies on early explorer peoples include Donald B. Harden, *The Phoenicians* (1980); Patrick Vinton Kirch, *The Lapita Peoples: Ancestors of the Oceanic World* (1997); and Simon James, *Exploring the World of the Celts* (1993, reprinted 2005). Two readable books on the Vikings are Gwen Jones, *A History of the Vikings*, 2nd ed. (2001); and P.H. Sawyer, *Kings and Vikings: Scandinavia and Europe, AD 700–1100* (1982, reprinted 1998).

There are many translations of Herodotus' *History*, one of the most up-to-date being Robin Waterfield (trans.), *The Histories*, new ed., edited by Carolyn Dewald (2008). Peter Green, *Alexander of Macedon, 356–323 BC*, rev. and enlarged (1974, reissued 1991), is a complete biography, with genealogy and an annotated bibliography; and Michael Wood, *In the Footsteps of Alexander the Great: A Journey from Greece to India* (1997, reissued 2004), is the companion volume to the popular BBC documentary series of the same name. Adrian Goldsworthy, *Caesar: Life of a Colossus* (2006), is a thorough treatment; and Ernle Bradford, *Julius Caesar: The Pursuit of Power* (1984), is a readable survey.

A classic English translation of Faxian's *Foguoji* by H.A. Giles is *The Travels of Fa-hsien* (1877, with many subsequent printings). René Grousset, *In the Footsteps of the Buddha* (1932, with many subsequent reprints; originally published in French, 1929), discusses the life of Chinese pilgrim Xuanzang against the background of Tang history and Buddhist philosophy. Much interesting information on al-Idrīsī is given in the introduction to S. Maqbul Ahmad (trans.), *India and the Neighbouring Territories in the Kitāb Nuzhat al-Mushtāq fiʿKhtirāq al-ʿAfāq* (1960), an English translation of a part of al-Idrīsī's work. There are several English translations of the *Secret History*, the most accessible being *The Secret History of the Mongols: The Life and Times of Chinggis Khan*, new ed., trans. and ed. and with an introduction by Urgunge Onon (2000). Leo de Hartog, *Genghis Khan, Conqueror of the World* (1989, reissued 2005; originally published in Dutch, 1979), emphasizes the military strategy and foresight of the ruler.

Christopher Dawson (ed.), *The Mongol Mission* (1955, reprinted as *Mission to Asia*, 1980), includes information on Giovanni Da Pian Del Carpini and other 13th- and 14th-century missionaries to Mongolia and China. A modern, readable, and dependable version in English of Marco Polo's work is Ronald Latham (trans.), *The Travels of Marco Polo* (1958), available in many later editions; and one of the best studies of Polo, his journeys, his book, and his times is John Larner, *Marco Polo and the Discovery of the World* (1999). *The Adventures of Ibn Battuta: A Muslim Traveler of the 14th Century*, rev. ed. (2005), is a scholarly though readable biography.(Arabic Ṣaydā) Külek Boğazi) Sīwah Shāhrūd Āmol Nad-e ʿAl Vazīrābād qayṣar Hossō (Arabic Ṣaydā) Külek Boğazi) Sīwah Shāhrūd Āmol Nad-e ʿAl Vazīrābād qayṣar Hossō al-Masʿūdī al-Ḥusayn Kitāb al-awsaṭ al-Fusṭāṭ Muḥammad

INDEX